Is It Time to Start Exporting to Europe?

LESSONS LEARNT FROM EXPORTERS GLOBALLY

Christelle Damiens

Also by Christelle Damiens

The 4 Steps to Generate Your First Million Euros in Sales
WINNER BEST COMMUNICATIONS AND SALES BOOK, 2020
Smart WFM Australian Business Book Awards

Ready, Tech, Go! The Definitive Guide to Exporting Australian Technology to Europe, 2016
Amazon Bestseller

Contents

Preface

A new world of opportunity

There is no doubt that doing business overseas is so much easier now than it was just five years ago. One of the major enablers of international business has been technology. It has allowed easier and faster access to buyers all across the globe. You can now get to know your customers even if you have never met them face to face. And you don't have to meet your customers in person to close a deal. You have the ability to work more efficiently and collaboratively with your customers' teams and to support them remotely. You also can create global online customer communities. Marketing teams can target international customers and segment their profiles, which was often not possible or was very expensive before social media.

ABOUT THIS BOOK

Today, exporting is heavily reliant on a business being able to connect with customers digitally. Exporting can happen at a faster pace if you are able to take advantage of this capability. This acceleration is an opportunity to leverage for agile businesses, and this is exciting.

I would like to welcome you to a world of opportunities that will arise from reading this book. Let me guide you through this new world. In part I, we will uncover some of the key recent trends that impact exporters; what I call the 'new state of exporting'. Major disruptions such as a global pandemic, geopolitical tensions and radical trends mean we have to be ready to adapt, shift and change. Flexible and agile businesses always thrive. **I will provide examples of these disruptions and reasons why we need to be agile to adapt our business to them.** One major lesson to learn from a global pandemic is you should future-proof your business by having diversified export destinations. Relying solely on your domestic market or on a limited number of export destinations is a risk. Being agile and able to get sales from several countries definitely helps to keep revenue flowing in the business. In this book, we will look specifically at Europe and why this diverse market is a great place to export to. In the second half of part I, I will explain **why Europe is a great export market for non-European businesses. I will look at macro trends and also outline specific opportunities right now in the European market for agile businesses.**

Given we are in a disrupted, fast-paced environment, there is one certainty we can hang on to. **We need to learn from those that have gone before us.** And this is what the rest of the book will focus on. In part II, **I will introduce you to the businesses I curated** for this book. They are at different stages in their internationalization phase and bring a wealth of experience.

Let me first explain why I think listening to others that have gone through the export to Europe journey is important.

First, I would like to share with you a McKinsey article's wisdom about market entry. (I strongly recommend you read the full article.[1])

---

1   'Beating the Odds in Market Entry: How to avoid cognitive biases that undermine market entry decisions,' John T. Horn, Dan P. Lovallo, S. Patrick Viguerie, 2005, www.mckinsey.com/capabilities/strategy-and-corporate-finance/our-insights/beating-the-odds-in-market-entry.

According to this article, '**the annals of business history report that for every successful market entry, about four fail**.' And this happens equally to start-ups, large corporations and highly skilled entrepreneurs. This is mainly due to cognitive bias. One of the main reasons argued in this article is that executives only rely on their internal views to make decisions. Failure to look at outside views to make a specific decision leads to failure. What the McKinsey article proposes instead is to form a 'reference class: a group of similar decisions that other companies have made in the past'.

One of the recommendations provided is to look at not only successful entries but also failed ones: 'The greater the overlap with the experience of the industry in question, the more valuable each example for the reference class.'

For this book, I have collected stories of exporters from around the world. The objective is to remove blind spots for any newcomer to the European market. Their sharing of their export stories is genuine and generous, and this is what makes the lessons learnt so valuable for other businesses.

For small and medium-sized companies, failure in the European market is very costly. In some cases, it can even push a business to bankruptcy. One of our customers went through this roller-coaster. They obtained their European regulatory approval, hired a salesperson in the UK, started to target multiple European countries, conducted a number of European shows . . . and two years down the track, they had no sales. The business almost went bankrupt.

A couple of years ago, another of our customers admitted to us that they had made a very bad decision in their early days in the European market. They had recruited early on a senior executive based in Germany. This senior executive underperformed, and when it came time to dismiss him, they had to pay him a redundancy fee of €250,000. Needless to say, it was a very high cost for a small business.

Stephen McIntyre in a February 2021 article published in *Harvard Business Review* shares that even the most successful US software firms make costly mistakes when venturing overseas.[2] He mentions four common mistakes:

- The first mistake is going overseas at the wrong time (too soon or too late).

- The second mistake he mentions is what he calls 'success amnesia'. In other words, companies forget how hard they worked to get their business off the ground, and they underestimate the task of doing the same in Europe.

- The third mistake is to select the wrong first hire who has no prior knowledge of Europe.

- The fourth mistake is when the CEO is over-delegating and is not attuned enough to the European side of the business and is not giving enough attention to this growth opportunity.

'Exporting' is a great word, however in the current state of exporting it almost feels outdated. The Oxford Dictionary definition of exporting is 'to send out goods or services for sale in another country.'[3] It comes from Latin, composed of the verb to carry – 'portare' – and out of or from – 'ex'.[4] This word captures the basic concept of exporting, but it does not capture the many new facets of modern exporting. Modern ways of operating a business in a global market have completely redefined this concept. Exporters don't only ship goods they have manufactured; they may not ship goods at all. A software business selling online access to cloud-based software to overseas customers is an exporter. You can also argue that a service business setting up a team in Europe to deliver

---

2   'What U.S. Startups Get Wrong About Expanding into Europe,' Stephen McIntyre, www.hbr.org/2021/02/what-u-s-startups-get-wrong-about-expanding-into-europe.

3   *Oxford English Reference Dictionary*, 2003 Edition.

4   *Dictionnaire Gafflot*, Latin-Francais.

the service in this market is also an exporter. The traditional concept of shipping boxes is dead, particularly in business to business. Interesting exporters with diverse profiles (manufacturers, software developers, service providers) have developed amazing ways to expand their customer base internationally. Best practices can and should be learnt from other types of businesses. This is why this book is a journey of learning through export stories from a diverse range of exporters.

These are the reasons it is crucial to learn from others: it will save your business time and money. This is why I will share the experiences of eight companies from different countries who genuinely shared their experience of entering the European market. So, after an introduction of your devoted author and to the businesses, I will take you through their entry strategies in part II. And in the last chapter of the book, I am sure you are going to enjoy the best lessons they learnt on their journey.

ABOUT ME

First, I would like to share with you where I come from. I will let you in my personal story to give you a bit of background. I come from a very multicultural background. I was born in France, from Italian descendants on my mother's side, and my dad gave me a French family tree. My mother's family, originally from Italy, migrated to North Africa to work in the mines. At the end of the colonial period, their descendants came back to Europe and settled in France, Italy and Germany. Part of the family stayed and still lives in Tunisia today. It created a very intriguing family background as a kid and it fascinated me as I grew up. From there, I always played the role of the bridge between different family branches. It motivated me to learn German as a first foreign language. It also pushed me to find my first job at 13 to pay for a ticket to meet my family in Tunisia. And from there, I never stopped. This is why I am quite agile, respectful and passionate about navigating a cross-cultural environment.

As a consequence, international business and export came naturally to me. I was always drawn to it. From the age of 17, I studied and worked in Austria, the UK, Germany, Italy, India and Australia. After multiple export experiences in Europe in the early years of my career, through to a longer sales career at IBM selling to very large French multinationals in banking and insurance, I knew I would always work in sales. As I migrated at the age of 29 to Australia from France, one of the reasons for creating my business Exportia was my love for international sales. And I did what a lot of business advisors advise against: I created a job for myself. Later I realized I actually had a business in my hands. But this story is for another book!

A European corporate experience for a US tech giant was a foundational experience, showing how European corporate large-deal-making works, and also taught me that even giants get it wrong when adapting their approach to a specific European market. I remember the struggle to get our marketing to translate marketing slide decks for new product launches to French. And everyone in the business doing their own French slide decks! What a waste of time!

This life journey – I am mid-40s now – gave me the joy and pride and challenging task of taking close to 100 high-growth, small and medium-sized technology-based non-European businesses to the European market in 17 years, with products or services that ranged from medical devices, to biotechnologies, to machinery, to safety, to electronics, to cloud-based software and more. We have dealt in GreenTech, AgTech, EdTech, MedTech – any industry you can add 'tech' to.

The Exportia Manifesto

Through my business and thanks to the companies interviewed for this book as well, I can see that businesses – regardless of whether they are from Australia, New Zealand, the US, Canada, Korea, Japan, Taiwan or India – tend to make the same mistakes. On the other hand, successful companies tend to always succeed for the same reasons. And there are deep trends that every exporter should consider in their journey to the European market.

Therefore, when I look back at my 23 years of business development in Europe, 17 years of working with non-European exporters from around the world in Europe, and having been literally on the frontline of a pandemic and experiencing the deep changes from there, I think it's really important that non-European exporters walk away from this book with clarity on what really matters.

If there were only six elements that the non-European exporters from around the world should implement to succeed in Europe, it would be these:

1. Go green to succeed in Europe

The European Green Deal has a most ambitious sustainability target. And it already filters through the entire business ecosystem. Every European customer of yours will ask you to demonstrate your green credentials. They are held accountable by their government, their board and their employees. As a supplier to them you are part of their carbon footprint, and you must show how – as a bare minimum – you don't negatively impact their green target.

2. Focus is key to success

It's a temptation that is hard to resist, going everywhere and being on every front. The glamorous Paris, London, Berlin, Milan at the bottom of your website, or on your business card. But truth is, success only happens when teams are focused on one European country at a time. And this country needs to combine two characteristics: it must be one of your largest total addressable markets; and this country must have an appetite for your product (you need to have tested the interest). From there, building traction will be easier. You should also stick to one specific industry where you already have traction in any other part of the world.

In some specific cases, a great move might even be to focus on just one region within your focus country first, if you are aware that a given region provides access to a good share of your total addressable market. It is easier to create traction in a smaller geographical area, and just within one specific industry. The word of mouth travels faster within a smaller network.

3. Generate sales before you set up an office or hire

Europe is composed of a mosaic of countries and languages. Sales can be generated without having a local entity. Generating sales in your focus country will enable you to hire the right talent to support further sales growth in this country. Do not hire before you have initial traction. You need to make sure your investment is allocated in the right country and the right person. This is how fast sales happen. Otherwise, you will end up hiring a Spaniard to grow France or a Brit for Germany and it will take much longer to get sales results than having a French person for the French market and a German for Germany.

4. Plug in to ecosystems larger than yours

Now you may be wondering, how do I get sales started without hiring!? One of the best ways to do so as an unknown business in the market is to build a local ecosystem. Your local ecosystem will mainly be built on an efficient sales channel or distribution network.

If they have the right customer base, the right set of skills and the right motivation, your channel partner or distributor will give you fast access to your desired customer base. They will have existing commercial relationships with your target customers. They have sales reps who talk to them and sell to them on a daily basis. Many corporates will feel much more comfortable buying from their current partner, rather than from an unknown business that is coming from outside the European Union. If you support your ecosystem well and you show them how to sell your offerings and you have a track record to demonstrate you will support the sales, you will succeed.

5. Spend time building your first European anchor customers

Even if you build an ecosystem and have set up a strong channel partner or distribution network, it's vital for your business to build direct relationships with key European customers. In the initial stages, these anchor customers will enable you to grow your sales in a specific industry, in a specific region, or even in a given country if they are quite influential. And once they have adopted your product and you have made sure they are 100% satisfied, they will enable you to take the pulse of the market, they will provide feedback for you to continuously improve your product and your systems, and they will suggest new features. These anchor customers will come on board if you have decreased their cost of switching to your business, and if you have overcome every concern they had about adopting your solution or the reluctance they had to buy from you as an unknown entity. Every concern a customer has about buying from you is a lever you can pull to get access to closing a sale. Your first anchor customers are going to be the local credentials you will need to build your European market. They need to be treated like royalty.

6. Stay agile by continuously learning

As you build sales one country at a time via a channel partner network and relying on a solid base of anchor customers, you will continuously learn about each European country and your market. Agility is what is going to allow you to adapt and refine your strategy to achieve better business outcomes.

Part I

The new state of exporting

First we will look at key trends that deeply affect international business and exporters. We will start with e-commerce, we will then go through the unexpected impact of the global pandemic on businesses, and we will look at the geopolitical climate, notably the war in Ukraine. We will also analyze the rising cost of freight and its impact on Europe and on exporting to Europe. We will also examine Brexit and what it means for Britain and also for exporters to Europe. I have also included an interview to capture the critical need to stay agile as exporters.

Then we will have a close look at Europe at the macroeconomic level, considering the current state of trade agreements within the European Union. I will also comment on some of the key investments the European Union is making. We will then look at specific opportunities that are currently available in Europe for non-European businesses.

Chapter 1

The key trends impacting exporters

ACCELERATION OF THE ADOPTION OF E-COMMERCE

This is our first trend. E-commerce is nothing new, but it has flourished in recent years, providing the opportunity to maintain continuous operations and for customers to buy goods and services from the comfort of their homes and at their leisure 24/7.

EuroCommerce, the European Industry body for e-commerce, noted robust e-commerce growth over the past decade that accelerated during COVID-19, with 71% of the European Union population buying online in 2020 – it was only 64% in 2018.[5]

A report from the OECD observes that this trend will stay in the long term, now that businesses have invested in this new sales channel.[6] Consumers have adopted this new purchasing habit and it's very unlikely they will give up this convenient way of shopping. The report

---

5   '2021 European E-commerce Report,' Light Version, page 3, www.ecommerce-europe.eu/publication/2021-european-e-commerce-report-light-version.

6   'E-commerce in the Time of COVID-19,' www.oecd.org/coronavirus/policy-responses/e-commerce-in-the-time-of-covid-19-3a2b78e8/.

also underlines that e-commerce sites are likely to retain their shoppers through loyalty programs.

In Europe and the UK, e-commerce was already undergoing double-digit growth before the pandemic, and this growth accelerated from 2020 (an increase of 30% for EU-27 countries in April 2020 compared to April 2019 for retail sales via the internet or via mail order houses). According to the OECD, in the United Kingdom the share of e-commerce in retail rose from 17.3% to 20.3% between the first quarter of 2018 and the first quarter of 2020, to then rise significantly to 31.3% between the first and second quarter of 2020. It's interesting to note that in the following graph, the US had slower growth for the same period – between 10% and 15%.

US and UK e-commerce growth 2018–20[7]

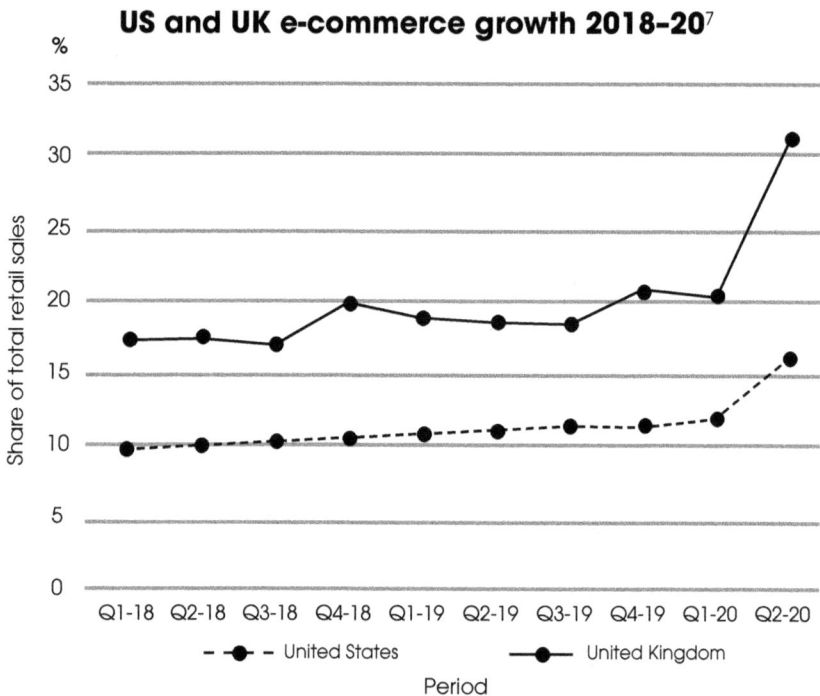

---

7   'E-commerce in the Time of COVID-19,' OECD report. For full details go to: www.oecd.org/coronavirus/policy-responses/e-commerce-in-the-time-of-covid-19-3a2b78e8.

In Europe and the UK, several government and private initiatives have been observed according to the OECD report. For example, eBay UK dropped their fees temporarily to enable better access to e-commerce for SMEs.

What I also find interesting is the opportunity for non-European companies to use e-commerce as a channel to enter the European market. The '2021 European E-commerce Report' found that a fair share of online purchases happen via sellers from non-EU countries.[8] Overall, in the EU-27 countries in the last three months of 2020, 22% of e-commerce purchases were done via sellers from non-EU countries. It means that e-commerce is definitively a channel to consider seriously.

While in recent years the e-commerce trend has been driven by B2C, there are clear signs that B2B transactions are more and more done online. It has taken a little longer for B2B to embrace e-commerce, but the pandemic acceleration has deeply engrained this new habit. It means consumers who may also happen to be professionals, employees or business owners are now expecting to be able to buy online for their professional use. And they also search for products online. In the same report, it is interesting to note that the figures show this trend: 43% of large businesses of 250 or more employees have e-commerce sales. There is also a good share of SMEs having e-commerce sales, with 20%.[9] It shows that European companies are fully embracing the sales channel of e-commerce. It should be a great sales enabler for any non-EU business entering the European market. Businesses are very optimistic about the growth of e-commerce in their sales, as you can see in the following graph.

8 '2021 European E-commerce Report,' Light Version, page 15, www.ecommerce-europe.eu/publication/2021-european-e-commerce-report-light-version.

9 SMEs are considered to have between 10 and 249 persons employed.

The key trends impacting exporters

**European B2B sellers' expectations of
e-commerce growth through 2025**[10]

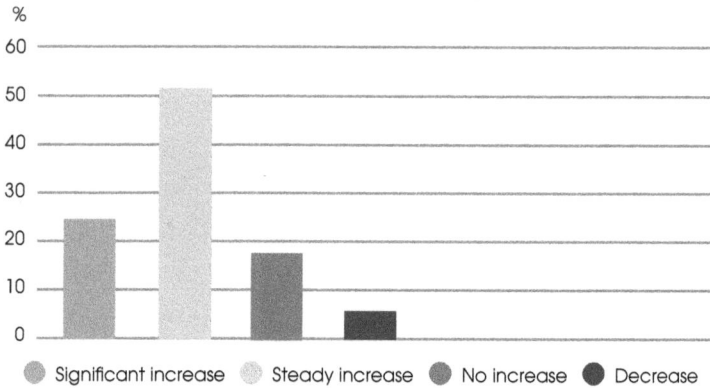

Source: International Trade Administration

As the European Union wishes to make sure the VAT (value-added tax) is paid in all e-commerce transactions, it has created a portal called the One-Stop Shop. It facilitates compliance with VAT rules for imported goods. It has been in place since July 1, 2021. You must check this out and ensure you are meeting your tax obligations when implementing your e-commerce site.

Broad adoption of video conferencing and adaptation of sales processes

E-commerce is a trend that mainly involves business to consumers (B2C), but what about B2B in Europe? In Europe, digital purchases go beyond household purchases, according to a McKinsey report.[11] Many industry sectors have embraced the delivery of their services without face-to-face meetings and instead are using telephone or video calls.

---

10 International Trade Administration data, www.digitalcommerce360. com/2022/03/29/b2b-ecommerce-in-europe-nears-a-milestone.

11 'How European Businesses can Position Themselves for Recovery,' Tera Allas, Pal Erik Sjatil, Sebastien Stern, Exkart Windhagen, www.mckinsey.com/industries/ public-and-social-sector/our-insights/how-european-businesses-can-position-themselves-for-recovery.

Healthcare institutions, education and entertainment have fully embraced this trend. Charité, a university hospital in Berlin, offers consultations via a new online video clinic. The Berlin State Opera broadcast March of Geister to 160,000 online viewers. Nightclubs have shifted to stay-at-home parties. Schools and universities have shifted to online teaching.

The adoption of video conferencing has accelerated sharply to support this new digital way of doing business, with downloads of webapps in European countries estimated to have increased 10 to 30 times since March 2019.

Professional services are prime adopters of this mode of delivery, as a lot of export services can effectively be delivered without the supplier or the customer crossing any borders. This sharp trend in professional services is here to stay. Severe travel restrictions in Europe have accelerated this trend, and time and travel cost savings are a great incentive for it to continue in post-pandemic times.

Professional services have the capability to be quite agile in their way of transforming the delivery of services to benefit from video conferencing capabilities. But I also would like to underline the agility of manufacturers in adapting their sales processes to an online world and away from traditional face to face. This is an important trend for manufacturers from non-EU countries to embrace to bulletproof their success – whether there is a pandemic or not. When working with small and medium-sized manufacturers in my business Exportia, we have constantly been challenged to sell without physically visiting a European customer to demonstrate a product or convince a potential buyer. We have had to challenge our customers to adjust their sales process to ensure we could close sales. It has involved reassuring the European customer that our customer was a reliable supplier, even if there was no face-to-face meeting. It meant we had to demonstrate the credibility of our customer through their current contracts with large multinationals or government organizations. The other part we often had to do in the B2B sales process was to introduce or finetune a trial phase of the new product or solution to be able to sell. That would involve sending samples to test along with the commitment to provide formalized feedback, product try and buys, or other methods to get the European customers comfortable buying from a new non-European manufacturer. This has been made possible – as highlighted by the McKinsey report – by a broad adoption by European firms of video conferencing. In this way, manufacturers have also benefited from time and travel cost savings. And for many of them the transformation and the efficiency gains achieved during the pandemic are here to stay.

This trend is highly beneficial to new entrants into the European market.

THE RISE OF ONLINE COMMUNITIES AS A TOOL TO INCREASE EXPORTS

Realizing that e-commerce is not just for selling to consumers but also an opportunity for businesses to sell to businesses also applies to online communities. It's not just for consumers or private households anymore! A new world of opportunities for businesses to create online communities is becoming more prominent. And in the case of a non-European business entering the European market, this is a great way to get to know your market, to gather their feedback if you launch a new product, to encourage them to engage with your business more often, to check in with their use of your product, and to collate some market feedback. Meurer et al.'s study from 2022 shows that online communities help entrepreneurs in times of uncertainty.[12] I think this extract from the study is key:

---

12 Meurer, M.M., Waldkirch, M., Schou, P.K. et al. 'Digital Affordances: How entrepreneurs access support in online communities during the COVID-19 pandemic,' *Small Bus Econ* 58, 637–663 (2022). www.doi.org/10.1007/s11187-021-00540-2.

(1) Online communities can help resolve problems and collect critical resources in times of crisis, such as digital marketing tools to compensate client loss.

(2) Online communities can support entrepreneurs to waterproof ideas in early venture stages through feasibility checks so that entrepreneurs can better evaluate opportunities.

(3) Online communities can help understand and reflect on new emerging topics, such as work from home.

(4) Online communities can provide tailor-made plans for entrepreneurs by engaging in frequent interaction with support seekers.

Taken together, online communities can assist entrepreneurs in their actions which are especially important in times of great uncertainty.

The rise of online communities creates another way to power exports and bridge the gap of distance with customers across the globe.

THE GOOD OLD CONCEPT OF TRUST IN BUSINESS

In many parts of the world, including Europe, global supply chains have been disrupted and factories have been constrained to stop supplying to overseas markets. This has created a climate of distrust among European buyers. According to IBISWorld, Asian suppliers have failed a number of global customers, so these customers are now looking at diversifying their supply: 'If the COVID-19 outbreak curtailed output across Asian factories, some Australian producers may benefit from enhanced export opportunities as global markets seek out alternative suppliers.'[13]

---

13 'IBISWorld Report,' Update August 2020.

Generally speaking, any non-European business entering the European market will have to put extra effort in to building trust with buyers. They are going to have to demonstrate how reliable they are in their supply chain. I have seen very detailed questionnaires to suppliers on this topic. A new supplier will also have to demonstrate how closely they are going to support their European customers.

And something that is very important to a European mindset: are you going to be here for us in the long run? Building or restoring trust with customers is a key trend that should not be underestimated by new entrants to the European market.

GEOPOLITICS HAS CREATED TENSIONS

The war in Ukraine has reinforced the need for European businesses to futureproof themselves. In the energy sector, some of the European economies have had to revert to coal to minimize the impact of reduced gas imports from Russia.

This conflict highlights the urgency for countries to increase their independence in terms of energy and the importance of not relying on fossil fuels. The objective for Europe to be the first economy with net-zero greenhouse gas emissions by 2050 remains. To tackle this objective, technologies to support greener buildings, sustainable farming, carbon neutral transport, energy efficiency and increased biodiversity will still be at the top of European companies' priorities.

Geopolitics has a direct impact on which industry sector to tackle first. Some sectors are less affected than others. As a small business it is helpful for you to be aware of this as you are preparing your entry into the European market. As per an analysis by the European Central Bank published in the *ECB Economic Bulletin* in its April 2022 issue, savings are rising, consumption is moderately affected, while business investment decisions are affected to a larger extent.[14] This is shown in the following graph. What it means for businesses entering the European market in this current context is that buyers will look twice before they make a capital equipment investment; they will see if they can keep using their current equipment or find another solution instead. It means you are going to have to show a return on investment and be competitive. Consumption has decreased but to a lower extent, while household savings has increased.

The European Central Bank data also shows that consumption of non-durable goods is less negatively impacted than durable goods. In terms of sectors, the service industry is significantly less impacted than the manufacturing sector. For businesses that can tackle multiple industries, you may have to reshuffle your target sectors and how you prioritize them based on this trend.

Macroeconomic impact of Russia's invasion of Ukraine[15]

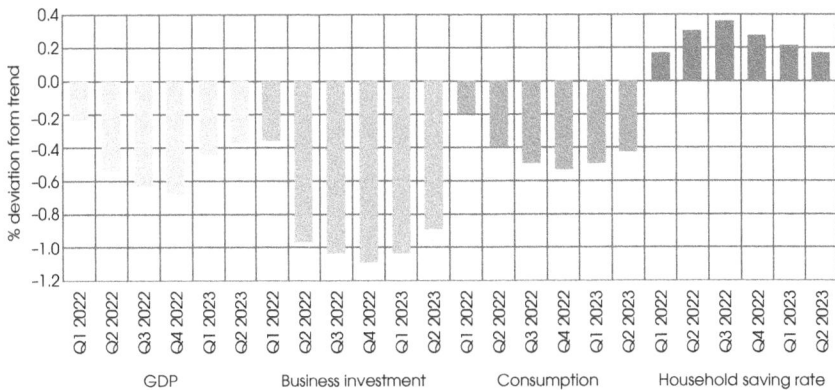

The key trends impacting exporters

14 'The Impact of the Russian Invasion of Ukraine on Euro Area Activity via the Uncertainty Channel,' Prepared by Alina Bobasu and Roberto A. De Santis, *ECB Economic Bulletin*, Issue 4/2022, www.ecb.europa.eu/pub/economic-bulletin/focus/2022/html/ecb.ebbox202204_02~b5e18e967d.fr.html.

15 Ibid.

Now that we have learnt the hard way – with our first global 21st century pandemic and a major war breaking out – that our businesses need to be agile, only businesses that stay on the front foot will succeed and maintain their edge.

The impact of the war in Ukraine for your exports to Europe

If we leave aside for a moment the human atrocity of having one more war on this planet, and be grateful that the topic of this paragraph feels a bit petty in comparison to what those populations are experiencing – let's proceed.

The International Monetary Fund outlines in an article published in 2022 the three major impacts of the Ukraine–Russia war for the global economy:

- The first impact is higher prices, mainly driven by commodities such as food and energy. This increases inflation. What it means for an exporter to the European markets is that European households have less money to spend and this will decrease demand.

- The second effect is that neighboring economies have to cope with disruptions to their supply chains and transfers of funds, and have to manage the arrival of refugees.

- The third effect is an erosion of business confidence.[16]

European economies are significantly affected by the pressure on imports of natural gas, of which Russia is the main supplier. This creates rising inflation. In addition, the recovery from the pandemic may be

---

16 'How War In Ukraine Is Reverberating Across World's Regions,' Alfred Kammer, Jihad Azour, Abebe Aemro Selassie, Ilan Goldfajn, Changyong Rhee, March 15, 2022, www.imf.org/en/Blogs/Articles/2022/03/15/blog-how-war-in-ukraine-is-reverberating-across-worlds-regions-031522.

slowed due to supply chain disruptions and as European economies increase their budget allocation to energy security and defense. Eastern European countries are the most exposed in the region, as they have seen the largest arrivals of refugees (three million) and the most supply chain disruptions.

However, generally the IMF article underlines that 'most European banks have modest and manageable direct exposures to Russia.'

THE COST OF FREIGHT HAS NEVER BEEN SO HIGH – WILL IT EVER GO DOWN?

An article published by the European Central Bank provides a great insight on the cause of the surge in freight costs. It was published in March 2021.[17] As the coronavirus started to come under control and manufacturing started to rise globally, many supply chain bottlenecks developed. China was one of the first countries to get back to normal in the first half of 2020. Chinese exports were then fueled by a need for intermediate goods, which increased the demand for container shipments. Shortages in containers have created more bottlenecks and contributed to an increase in shipping costs. Due to an uneven recovery of trade, containers were stuck in some locations while in high demand in other ports, contributing to surges in costs. Asian companies had to pay premium rates to get the containers back.

Other factors that contributed to the surge in freight costs are:

- the rising costs of fuel, which had an impact on shipping costs

17 'What is Driving the Recent Surge in Shipping Costs?' Prepared by Maria Grazia Attinasi, Alina Bobasu and Rinalds Gerinovics, Published as part of the *ECB Economic Bulletin*, Issue 3/2021, www.ecb.europa.eu/pub/economic-bulletin/focus/2021/html/ ecb.ebbox202103_01~8ecbf2b17c.en.html.

- the inability of airfreight to compensate for the difficulties in seafreight, due to its own difficulty returning activity to pre-COVID levels (problems included multiple flight line cancellations and reduced personnel).

This article estimated that the cost of freight should be resolved as international trade returns to normal.

Record profits were registered by the main carriers. Profit increases in 2022 in comparison to 2021 are ranging from 84% to 1442% according to the September 2022 DHL market outlook. I doubt an industry that has been working on very low margins for decades will want to let this level of profitability go. This will certainly not help in reducing freight costs for exporters.

Some voices are being raised to alert that these super-profits do not reflect the difficulty of the industry overall, notably the road transport industry, which has suffered from rising fuel prices as well as increased labor and maintenance costs, with limited ability to pass this on.[18]

At the time of writing, there are still labor shortages, high energy and fuels costs and high inflation in Europe, which makes it quite hard to have a clear picture on the cost of freight. To make sense of the overall trend, I would like to mention a publication by the French Bureau of statistics[19]. In this publication, they collate and analyze regularly the cost of freight services paid by 2000 French companies with a reference base of 2015. It shows the cost of freight by mode of transport.

This first table shows the price evolution of freight in Q1 (January to March 2023). Three figures are interesting: the increase in the price of rail transport is high, at 9.4%. And you can see that the price of airfreight and seafreight fell dramatically, respectively –12.4% and –20%.

---

18 'Shipping Profits Validate Calls to Change Law,' Peter Anderson, www.bigrigs.com. au/2022/06/23/shipping-profits-validate-calls-to-change-law.

19 'Indices des prix du transport de fret et de l'entreposage au premier trimestre 2023,' No 557 Juin 2023. 'Index of the prices of freight transport and warehousing in the first quarter 2023 (January to March 2023),' Issue No. 557, June 2023, INSEE, www.statistiques.developpement-durable.gouv.fr/publicationweb/557.

Price evolution of freight transport Q1 2023

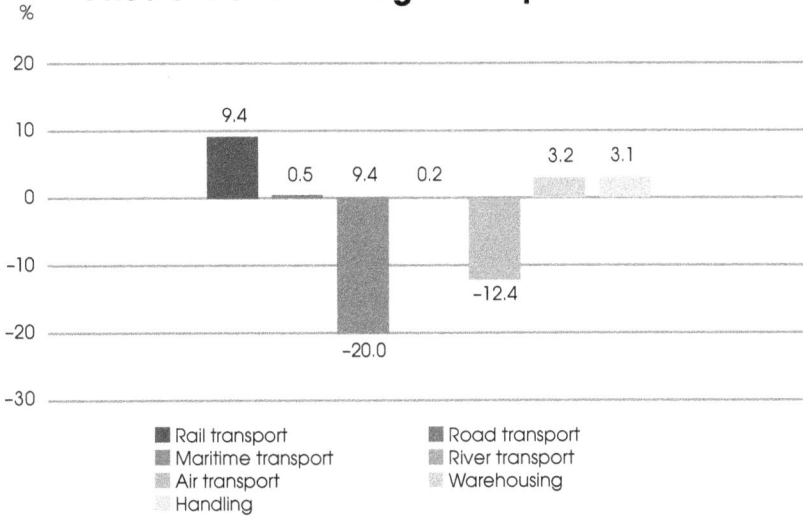

%

20

10

9.4

0.5   9.4   0.2

3.2   3.1

0

-10

-12.4

-20

-20.0

-30

■ Rail transport   ■ Road transport
■ Maritime transport   ■ River transport
■ Air transport   ■ Warehousing
■ Handling

The next two graphs give a longer view of what is happening. Let's look at freight rail transport and road. In the first quarter 2023, we had a drastic price increase in rail transport mainly due to the sharp rise of electricity, which has a direct impact on cost due to the power needed for convoys. And you can see there is a continuous increase in road freight transport prices since the first quarter 2023.

Now let's look at the trend presented by INSEE for seafreight and airfreight, which is what most non-European exporters would be mainly interested in. We note two consecutive price drops of airfreight prices by –4.6% in Q4 2022 (October to December 2022) and by –12.4% Q1 2023 (January to March).

And you can see a massive fall in the price of seafreight transport for two consecutive quarters as well: by –22.9% in Q4 2022 (October to December 2022) and by –20% Q1 2023 (January to March). INSEE argues that it is mainly due to a decrease in the tension of the transport capacity, and in the demand for seafreight transport.

Rail and road transport price increase

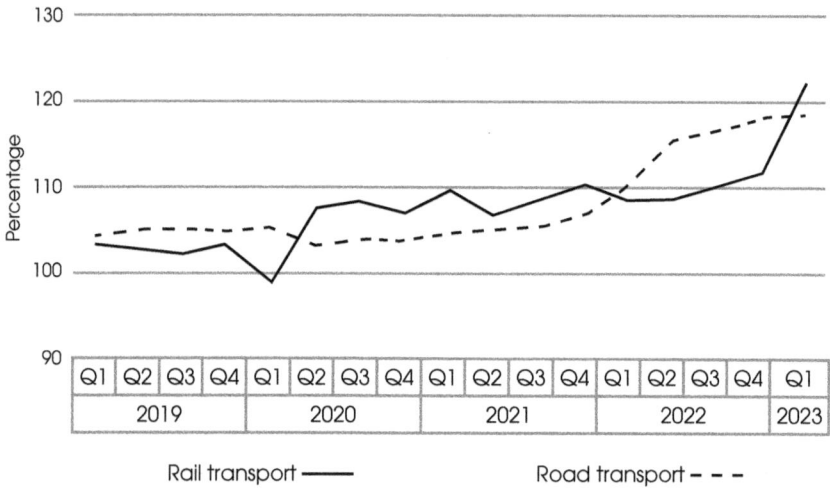

	Q1	Q2	Q3	Q4	Q1	Q2	Q3	Q4	Q1	Q2	Q3	Q4	Q1	Q2	Q3	Q4	Q1
	2019				2020				2021				2022				2023

Rail transport ——   Road transport − − −

Price index of maritime, river and air freight transport*

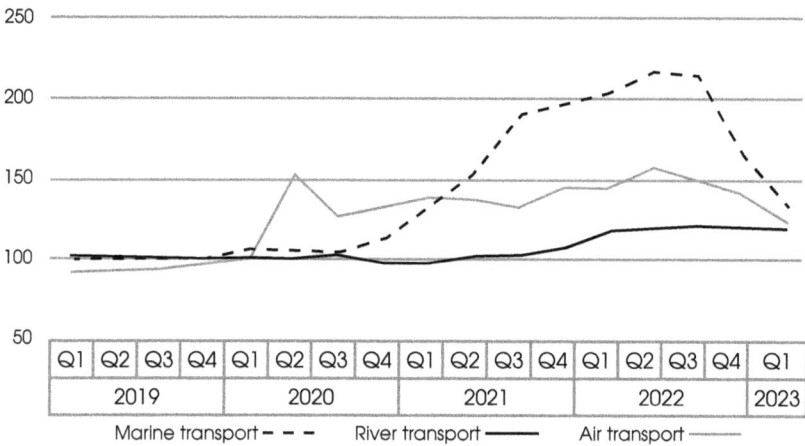

	Q1	Q2	Q3	Q4	Q1	Q2	Q3	Q4	Q1	Q2	Q3	Q4	Q1	Q2	Q3	Q4	Q1
	2019				2020				2021				2022				2023

Marine transport − − −   River transport ——   Air transport ——

* Reference: 100 in 2015.

What does that mean for exporters to Europe?

At the time of writing (late 2023), the cost of freight is still highly volatile and very hard to predict. A lot of European distributors and customers will therefore ask you to consider locking prices over time, switch to an INCOTERM that includes freight, or will ask you to offer free freight for large orders. In other words, they will try to pass on costs to their suppliers. That is where exporters, particularly small and medium-sized businesses, must be firm and protect their margins. It's important for your exports to exclude freight costs in pricing agreements.

In addition, the option of evaluating a European warehousing platform is something I would not have recommend looking at early on. But the high cost of freight and its volatility makes it more relevant to consider a third-party logistics provider (3PL) based in Europe. You would have the opportunity to optimize freight costs to a central platform that would then dispatch your goods within Europe.

THE ONGOING EFFECTS OF BREXIT

The United Kingdom is in a transition period as it has been hit by both Brexit and COVID-19.

Brexit is in full swing as I write, so the United Kingdom is now in a transition period. And this comes with challenges. One of them is labor shortages, due to some European Union workers going back to their home countries for visa reasons, including the precious resources of European lorry drivers and food factory workers. As a consequence, fuel and food shortages were encountered throughout 2021.[20] Europe is the most important source of food for Britons, with 30% of

20 'The Cause of Our Food and Petrol Shortages Is Brexit – Yet No One Dares Name It,' Jonathan Freedland, *The Guardian*, www.theguardian.com/commentisfree/2021/sep/24/food-petrol-shortages-brexit-goods-johnson-botched-deal.

all food eaten in the United Kingdom produced there, according to the British Retail Consortium.[21] In addition to transport challenges, the newly established custom clearance procedures have created more bottlenecks.

Financial services is a core industry in the United Kingdom. Due to Brexit, many financial services firms established in the UK have relocated their offices and staff to an EU-member country, where they have also transferred funds and assets. This very large move in financial services was highlighted in a New Financial report called 'Brexit & The City: The Impact So Far', which was published in April 2021.[22] This report highlighted that most of these moves were to Dublin (25%), then Paris (19%), then Luxemburg (17%), followed by Frankfurt (12%) and Amsterdam (12%). Since their first report published in March 2019, New Financial has seen a major acceleration in this trend.

What does it mean for your business?

In my business we have come across numerous challenges doing business in the UK in the last year or two (2020–21). This includes some of our distribution partners restructuring their organization, some having decided to move their European headquarters back to continental Europe, creating some issues and delays while trading with them. More broadly, businesses have generally postponed purchasing decisions as they have been hit by the double whammy of COVID and Brexit, which has made them cautious.

In addition, Britain leaving the EU means non-EU businesses will now have to go through a certification process for the UK separately from the European Union certification process, which has been dissuasive

---

21 CNN, edition.cnn.com/2021/09/14/business/brexit-uk-border-checks-delayed/index.html.

22 'Brexit & The City: The Impact So Far,' April 2021, www.newfinancial.org/brexit-the-city-the-impact-so-far.

for some companies that have preferred to focus on the European Union market.

Some of our customers who benefited from European subsidies to set up a company in Europe, and at the time established a UK head-quarters, have had to swiftly move their headquarters to the European Union to continue to benefit from the subsidies.

Companies from English-speaking countries have traditionally elected to establish their headquarters in the UK, because it's perceived as a safe haven. Commonwealth governments have commonalities in terms of legal frameworks and fiscal rules. This is not a sufficient reason anymore to automatically use the UK as a gateway for the rest of Europe. The size of the UK market and the need for a specific certifi-cation and import clearance make it harder to justify having a firm's European headquarters in the UK.

Radical changes

In recent years, the pace and depth of changes has been incredible and the changes so dramatic that they became irreversible. Exporters are at the forefront of these changes and have to constantly monitor the pulse. Radical changes have an enormous impact on business, as we have all witnessed with the global pandemic.

To highlight the necessity of staying agile, I asked a leading authority in the small business space, Andrew Griffiths, to relate to us his experience as he was delivering a business workshop to 1700 British businesses. The European Union had sponsored this program to assist small businesses transitioning through Brexit. His observations are really interesting and are useful for exporters to the European Union.

Could you please share the context and objective of the program?

In 2018 I was engaged to run a number of workshops around England, targeting small to medium businesses with the objective being to help them plan their international sales and marketing strategies in the lead up to Brexit. The workshop title that they wanted me to deliver was 'Branding Your Business for International Sales'. There were approximately 1700 businesses partaking in these workshops, from a broad and diverse range of industries right across England. Most had been exporting to Europe in some shape or format (which of course was relatively easy with England being a member of the European Union).

What was your mandate? What was the main area the EU wanted you to support?

This project was funded by the European Union as an initiative to help British businesses prepare for the impending and inevitable changes that were about to happen. The concern was that business in general in the UK was not prepared, they weren't planning strategically, and the general consensus was that it would be a disaster, particularly for smaller businesses (in this case small businesses being considered any operation up to about 1000 employees). The UK Government realized that the larger organizations were more able to engage professional advisors and consultants to help them transition, but small businesses were not in the same position. So in a day, I had to get them ready for the transition, a mighty task in reality.

What were the areas you planned to tackle - being a workshop about 'Branding Your Business for International Sales'?

I was really focusing on helping these businesses refine their brand to make it more appealing for international markets. So we were covering corporate imaging, language, key messages, the importance of online presence, researching the countries where they wanted to export and other topics like promotional material and making it easy for customers to buy from them.

Did you have to change your game plan during the course of the program? Why?

The first and most alarming realization I had was that most of the businesses attending the workshops had a complete lack of strategy about moving into a world where England was no longer a member of the European Union. They just wanted to keep selling to their existing markets, hoping things would not be that different. Of course this was not true. I was also surprised to see many of the businesses had no clear understanding about creating a compelling competitive advantage – or to put it simply, why should anyone buy what they are selling?

At the beginning of each workshop I would ask, which countries did they want to export to? The answer was always France and Germany as the first two priorities. And when I asked why they should buy from them, the only reason was that they were British. To me it was very clear there were two fundamental flaws here straight away. They wanted to export to the countries they just rejected as a nation, and their only compelling competitive advantage was that they were British.

When it came to looking to other countries or areas to export to, the two biggest responses were 'the Middle East' and 'China' – one because of proximity and perceived economic abundance and one simply because of its size. Anyone who has done any exporting to the Middle East as a region or China will know exactly how tough these two markets are. Having them as the fallback exporting target regions is a difficult strategy, and in many ways an unrealistic one to say the least. This complete lack of strategy was alarming, but it also made me realize we had to start there and everyone attending needed a very big reality check. That's when I realized why they had flown an Australian all the way to England to deliver these workshops. They knew I would call it the way it was, as Australians are known to do. So the biggest shift for me was to do exactly that. I had to be tough and explain, in a respectful way, that their strategy was not a strategy, it was a 'head in the sand' approach that would end badly. They were watching a major change hurtle towards them with no real plan to do anything about it. That was very concerning for me. I also realized that they didn't really want to hear what I had to say. Some did, many did not.

What lessons can small, medium and more generally high-growth businesses draw from your experience with the UK companies about to face the major change that is Brexit?

I think there are a number of key messages to take from this experience:

1. When it comes to exporting, conditions can change quite rapidly due to political issues. Never put all your eggs in the one basket.

2. Always be developing new markets to spread your risk.

3. When change is on the horizon, take action immediately. Don't wait for the change to arrive and then try to work your way through it.

4. Your compelling competitive advantage has to be relevant to the countries and the companies you want to deal with. As for this project, being British was not enough for any new market.

5. When it comes to looking for new markets, don't always assume the bigger markets are the best markets for you. Often it's better to go for smaller markets that are more aligned with you from a language perspective, where there is less competition, and you have cultural similarities.

Among these lessons, which one is particularly useful for exporters?

For me it's very easy to identify this – when change is on the horizon, take action immediately. Don't wait for the change to arrive and then try to work your way through it. Always be looking to new markets, doing your research, learning, planning, getting ready. Ask yourself this big question: what would you do right now if you were going to lose your biggest export market in six months?

THE IMPORTANCE OF BEING OPEN AND CHANGE-READY

Not just relying on your domestic market is crucial to staying in business for the long term. Equally important is the diversification of export markets.

New exporters must get started now. Businesses that are not exporting by now should have learnt the hard lessons of just relying on your domestic market. What if your local industry is struggling?

We also know that we need several export markets to minimize our risk. We have seen a new trend of protectionism increasing trade barriers into some destinations. For example, the Australian International Business Survey 2021 reported that 14% of exporters currently trading with the United Kingdom (on average) experience regulatory administrative barriers, and 35% of exporters currently trading with China (on average) experience regulatory administrative barriers.[23] This survey also highlighted an important fact: 'Businesses that exported to a wider range of markets performed better – 43% reported being financially better off compared to 12 months prior.' This is why Europe is a great destination to export to. The European Union is composed of a wide variety of countries, with diverse industries to target.

---

23 Australian International Business Survey 2021, www.export.org.au/eca-institute/ australias-international-business-survey-aibs-2021.

Chapter 2

Is it time to start exporting to Europe?

In this chapter I will provide several reasons for you and your management team to feel reassured that the European market is a great market to enter right now. I look at macro-economic aspects about Europe to start with. Then I will share some specific opportunities that I see as right for technology companies in Europe. We will then look at why Europe is easy to do business with, and even more so in recent years. I will also give you a tip, which will be particularly helpful if you are a business that is caring for the environment.

TRADE AGREEMENTS AND FREE TRADE AGREEMENTS

A free trade agreement (FTA) makes it easy for businesses to enter the European market – you don't have to worry about import duties![24] It also simplifies the process. Several countries currently have or are in

---

24 Agreements are shown listed on a map here: enterprise.gov.ie/en/what-we-do/ trade-investment/free-trade-agreements/. And you can find the latest agreements here: policy.trade.ec.europa.eu/eu-trade-relationships-country-and-region/ negotiations-and-agreements_en.

negotiation with the European union to finalize either a trade agreement or a free trade agreement, as shown in the following table.

Bilateral	Type of Agreement	Since	Details
EU–Korea (FTA had provisionally applied since July 2011 before it was formally ratified in December 2015.)[25]	Free trade	2015	This was the EU's first trade deal with an Asian country. It was also the EU's first FTA to include a chapter on trade and sustainable development. The chapter reaffirms the commitment of the EU and Korea to contribute to sustainable development by integrating labor and environmental (including climate) protection in the bilateral trade relationship.
EU–Japan	Economic partnership agreement	2019	Removed tariffs and other trade barriers and makes it easier for companies on both sides to import and export. The agreement removed the vast majority of duties paid by European and Japanese companies.

25 policy.trade.ec.europa.eu/eu-trade-relationships-country-and-region/countries-and-regions/south-korea_en.

Bilateral	Type of Agreement	Since	Details
EU–Australia[26]	To be determined	In negotiation	Aim of the negotiations: Remove barriers and help EU firms – especially smaller ones – to export more. Put European companies exporting to or doing business in Australia on an equal footing with those from countries that have signed up to the Trans-Pacific Partnership or other trade agreements with Australia.
EU–NZ	Trade agreement	2022	The European Union concluded negotiations for a comprehensive and ambitious trade agreement with New Zealand on June 30, 2022. Bilateral trade in goods between the two has risen steadily in recent years, reaching almost €7.8bn in 2021.[27]
EU–Canada	Comprehensive economic and trade agreement (CETA).	2017	Eliminates duties on 99% of all tariff lines.
EU–Singapore	Free trade agreement	2019	In 2023 a project was launched around establishing a digital trade agreement.

Is it time to start exporting to Europe?

26 policy.trade.ec.europa.eu/eu-trade-relationships-country-and-region/ countries-and-regions/australia/eu-australia-agreement_en.

27 policy.trade.ec.europa.eu/eu-trade-relationships-country-and-region/ countries-and-regions/new-zealand/eu-new-zealand-agreement_en.

EUROPEAN OPPORTUNITIES

European union investment plans

On the macroeconomic level in Europe, President of the European Commission Von der Leyen announced in July 2020 a very large stimulus plan of €750 billion, called NextGenerationEU. This scale of investment is unprecedented. The focus areas of this stimulus plan include modernization using artificial intelligence, industrial digitization, 5G and grid infrastructure. In addition, the EU will pursue a focus on the fight against climate change, particularly renewables, sustainable transport and energy efficient buildings.

If you are commercializing software or a machine that enables the automation of a manufacturing process or in the agricultural sector, your potential European customers are likely to be eligible for a grant on the purchase of your solution! This is a major opportunity for non-European businesses in digitization and automation.[28]

Europe is a great market for technology

As mentioned in the previous chapter, key trends showed progress in digitization in the European Union (pushed by the rise of e-commerce, telework, automation, and more labour mobility). The 2022 DESI (Digital Economy and Society Index) report reflects this major shift in digitization in Europe.[29]

% of customer interactions online	32% in Dec. 2019	55% in July 2020
% of fully digitized product or services provided by businesses	34% pre-COVID	50% during COVID
% businesses purchasing cloud-computing services	25% in 2019	41% in 2021

---

28 next-generation-eu.europa.eu/index_en.

29 digital-strategy.ec.europa.eu/en/policies/desi.

However, this report also indicates gaps, in terms of purchases of cloud computing. The main adopters were large corporates (72%) whereas only 40% of small and medium-sized businesses subscribed to cloud-computing services.

Many companies assumed they were 100% paperless, until their employees broadly adopted the home office megatrend for good. Many businesses came to the realization that paper files would have to go home with them. EU firms lag their US peers in terms of digitalization activities.[30] This creates opportunities for companies commercializing solutions to digitize documents and processes. Companies offering cloud-based solutions are best positioned to leverage this opportunity.

The other gap identified by the EU among member countries is the adoption of artificial intelligence and big data, which are still low, even in the most digitized economies. Finland, Denmark, the Netherlands, and Sweden are the most advanced countries in the European Union in terms of digitization.

European small businesses have been particularly vulnerable to cyber-attacks, and the same applies to large corporations and even to government departments and entire countries. The Defense editor of *The Economist* calls it the digital pandemic, whereby weak IT networks are infiltrated, and the organization's data is held hostage until a ransom is paid via cryptocurrency.[31] This major issue creates demand for cyber security, back-up solutions and other IT security solutions to educate the workforce to become even more vigilant with dubious emails and the like. Having a workforce at least partially working from home – which has now become the norm – creates more opportunities for hackers to get

Is it time to start exporting to Europe?

---

30 'Who is Prepared for the New Digital Age?' European Investment Bank, www.eib. org/en/publications-research/economics/surveys-data/eibis-digitalisation-report. htm.

31 'Hitting Back at Cyber-criminals: Until firms get the basics right, the digital pandemic will rage on,' Shashank Joshi, *The Economist*, The World Ahead 2022.

access to corporate data via mobiles, tablets and other private devices or poorly secured internet services.

On a more political front, the war in Ukraine reinforced the need in the EU for better cybersecurity to fight disinformation.

In this context, the European Union has formalized a plan to support digitization with concrete targets to be reached by 2030. There are four focus areas. The first one is increased skills in information and communications technologies (ICT), closing the gender gap in ICT, and reaching 80% of the population with basic digital skills. The other focus area is the digital business transformation of businesses, with two interesting priorities for exporters: the target to have 75% of EU companies using AI/big data and the cloud, and a specific target of 90% of SMEs to reach a basic level of digitization. Digitization of public services is also a focus, with a target of reaching 100% of key public services online. The other interesting target in the public sector is in e-health, with a target to enable 100% of EU citizens to have access to medical records online. A digital ID for every EU citizen is also a target for 2030.

To support the digitization progress of the EU, the last target is to set up a secure and sustainable infrastructure for the EU, with a target to provide gigabit internet speeds to everyone to enable better connectivity. An aggressive target is also to double the share of the EU in the global production of cutting-edge semi-conductors. By 2030, the objective is also to have the first quantum computer.

Multi-country projects have been approved; it's interesting which countries have agreed to collaborate in these, and on which specific projects.[32] For ICT businesses it's a great insight into which projects local players in each of these countries will have their eye on.

---

32 Refer to Table 1: Multi-country projects in the RRPs, Digital Economy and Society Index, www.knjiznice.si/wp-content/uploads/2023/01/DESI_Full_European_Analysis_2022.pdf.

Is reshoring a new trend in Europe that would prevent newcomers from succeeding in the European market? Not really!

The major trend of offshoring started in the 1970s, with large multi-nationals outsourcing some of their business processes, including manufacturing. These transnational companies coordinated directly or indirectly up to 80% of global value chains. The major beneficiary from this global trend was China, becoming a major destination for production offshoring as soon as it became a member of the World Trade Organization in 2001: 'One-third of global exports now originate from countries in the East Asia & Pacific region, particularly from China, compared to 18% in the 1980s (UN Comtrade, 2020).'[33]

This phenomenon created strong growth in international trade.

As the COVID-19 pandemic hit China, production facilities were shut down in a big way. It highlighted to the Western world its dependence on Chinese manufacturing. In addition, the rivalry between the US and China created political tensions and pushed increased protectionism on both sides.

As a result, the US, UK and Japanese economies have implemented policies to directly support reshoring production back within their own borders (Japan) or indirectly through promotion of innovation programs closer to home (US and UK).[34]

Reshoring is perceived as one of the major solutions to make nations less prone to shortages and less dependent on China. When considering the impact of reshoring for exporters to the European market, I wondered if this phenomenon was going to create barriers for non-EU companies to export to Europe. It does not seem to be the case.

---

33 'Post Covid-19 Value Chains: Options for reshoring production back to Europe in a globalised economy,' European Parliament, www.europarl.europa.eu/RegData/etudes/STUD/2021/653626/EXPO_STU(2021)653626_EN.pdf.

34 Ibid.

A study by the European Parliament published in March 2021 focused on the opportunity for the EU to establish programs to promote and establish reshoring within the European Union. The opportunities of nearshoring were also studied. The objective was to evaluate if the European market would be protected from shortages, and more broadly from global value chain shocks. Interestingly, this study not only highlighted that the COVID pandemic created disruptions in global value chains, but in addition other human-caused and natural shocks will have an impact.

So-called exogenous shocks such as natural disasters, pandemics and political conflicts as well as cyberattacks were identified as an increasing source of disruption of global value chains. However, reshoring to the EU as a major trend was judged as unlikely in the short and medium term. The only exception would be for geopolitical reasons. The European Union's strong push towards a green revolution in response to climate change will encourage shorter and regionalized value chains, according to the study. It was also identified that the COVID-19 pandemic highlighted that multilateral approaches to secure the free trade of critical products did not succeed, as each country established some level of protection to be able to supply its own critical products.

A European push for more automation creates opportunities for smart automation solution providers

In line with the above point about the intention of European members to increase their manufacturing base to reduce their dependency on global supply chains, the re-manufacturing goes along with the strong drive for automation and modernization of the manufacturing. European businesses are under pressure to automate their businesses rapidly to stay competitive in global markets.

The European Union has created programs to subsidize the transformation and modernization of its manufacturing industry. Key enabling technologies have been identified to support European industry, namely advanced manufacturing, advanced materials, life science technologies, micro/nano electronics and photonics, artificial intelligence, security and connectivity.

We have seen several examples. In France, subsidies were available for capital investment made by small and medium-sized businesses that were 20% of the investment.[35] It's interesting that the French priorities included additive fabrications, virtual or augmented reality, design software, and robotics.

There are also similar plans deployed by the Italian government to support the modernization and use of machinery in construction. And one of our US-based customers has been very successful in selling large capital equipment that automates and improves a specific task that would otherwise be very labour intensive, particularly in an industry where there are labour shortages.

Sustainable and ethical suppliers can gain market share in Europe to support European continuous effort

If you are at the forefront of sustainability and ethical business practices, you can really use this to differentiate your business and gain market share. European Union members and the UK are at the forefront of environmentally friendly practices, as demonstrated in their ranking in the Environmental Performance Index® calculated by Yale University. In fact, 27 European Union members are among the top 37 countries in the Environmental Performance Index®, the first 11 spots

35 www.economie.gouv.fr/plan-de-relance/mesures/aide-investissement-transformation-industrie-futur.

being occupied by European nations from 180 countries evaluated.[36] Environmental performance is a general concern shared by European nations, the UK included.

For any company entering the European market, it is also important to take into account the strong engagement of the European Union for a greener Europe. The EU has formed the ambitious goal of being the first carbon neutral continent by 2050. To support this goal, the objective is to reduce 55% of greenhouse gas emissions by 2030 (compared to 1990 levels).

To support the European Green Deal, the EU has developed policies and action plans in nine major areas:

- supplying clean, affordable and secure energy

- increasing the EU's climate ambition

- having a zero-pollution ambition by 2050

- preserving and restoring ecosystems and biodiversity

- accelerating the shift to sustainable mobility

- mobilizing industry for a clean and circular economy

- creating a fair, healthy and environmentally friendly food system

- building and renovating in an energy- and resource-efficient way

- leaving no one behind.[37]

This includes a target above 32% renewable energy as well as at least a 32.5% improvement in energy efficiency.

---

36 Wendling, Z. A., Emerson, J. W., de Sherbinin, A., Esty, D. C., et al. (2020). 2020 Environmental Performance Index, New Haven, CT: Yale Center for Environmental Law & Policy. epi.yale.edu.

37 assets.kpmg/content/dam/kpmg/xx/pdf/2021/11/green-deal-and-fit-for-55-slip-sheet_v5_web.pdf.

A long list of large multinationals have aligned themselves with these goals, including Shell, Total, BT, Henkel, Nestlé, LafargeHolcim, Novo Nordisk and Equinor.[38] At Exportia, during our multitude of conversations with European multinationals and notably in the course of a project organized for a delegation of 17 non-European businesses from APAC, we met the heads of innovation of nine multinationals and government departments in France. One of the top priorities was the reduction of carbon footprints and overall environmental impact. The other key theme was how to measure and track progress and report on their environmental scorecard. These were some of the solutions that multinationals were looking for.

In December 2022 the new Carbon Border Adjustment Mechanism was also announced.[39] This was put in place for carbon-intensive imports with the highest risk of carbon leakage, such as cement, iron, steel, aluminum, fertilizers, electricity and hydrogen. European companies importing these products from non-European companies now have to report greenhouse gas emissions embedded in their imports. This does not impact most of the readers of this book, but it shows the determination of the European Union to measure the impact of their imports in their carbon emissions.

Many climate action projects are currently being funded under Innovation Fund Projects by the European Union to accelerate the reduction of greenhouse gases.[40] These projects are small and large in scale, and they enable European companies to implement decarbonization projects: these projects are diverse, from carbon sequestration, to electrification of a furnace, to use of photovoltaic panels in agriculture. The list is long and is creating many opportunities for

---

38 carbon.ci/insights/companies-with-net-zero-targets/.

39 taxation-customs.ec.europa.eu/green-taxation-0/
    carbon-border-adjustment-mechanism_en.

40 List of projects: climate.ec.europa.eu/eu-action/funding-climate-action/
    innovation-fund/innovation-fund-projects_en.

non-European businesses to partner with European companies to share their expertise. There has never been a better time in this field.

THE EUROPEAN VIEW ON CORPORATE SOCIAL RESPONSIBILITY

Consumers and businesses are now craving honest and real engagement from businesses they are buying from. Businesses are expected to demonstrate corporate social responsibility (CSR) with their policies, and will also request their suppliers meet these standards as well. This practice has been in place for decades, but has accelerated in recent years, notably during the recent pandemic, when the world slowed down and has seen its effect on the environment. Deloitte has been monitoring this trend post-COVID and is confirming that this is continuing.[41]

As a non-European business dealing in the European market, the difficulty will lie in reliably demonstrating that your CSR standards meet your European consumers' standards. One way is to get a reliable and internationally recognized assessment done on your business. For example, Amfori is a Brussels-based not-for-profit organization that focuses on improving social and environmental performance in global supply chains.[42] They offer a range of programs for their members. One of the benefits of this organization is their global presence through their network of affiliates. Being a member and having been audited by one of these types of organizations offers a lot of credibility to companies.

On the simpler end of the spectrum, showing how you meet CSR standards is often a question of outlining your internal systems, processes

41 www2.deloitte.com/uk/en/pages/consumer-business/articles/sustainable-consumer.html.

42 www.amfori.org/content/amfori-bsci.

and affiliations. You can start by using as a guide what your European customers and distributors ask you to comply with.

Most important is being genuine in this matter and sharing all your initiatives.

What does this mean for you as a non-European company exporting to Europe?

As an exporter to the European Union you may aim to sell to multi-nationals, and as a consequence of becoming part of their supply chain you may be asked how you as a business are going to contribute positively to their environmental goals. In fact, in recent years, when negotiating with European distributors we have been asked more frequently to provide an environmental policy or to demonstrate how the businesses complied with theirs.

We have seen in our dealings with multiple large pan-European or global distributors active in Europe an interesting trend: the sustainability and ethical programs go beyond statements. For example, a global distributor in the laboratory sector is now offering green alternative products when their customers are buying. They are clearly highlighting these products as greener with a symbol. They are giving more visibility to the products that are less hazardous to the environment, that produce less waste, that are energy efficient, that can be disposed of in a sustainable way and are sustainably packaged. The request for sustainable packaging is a recurring one.

As we now all understand that we must be on board to protect our planet, most companies have naturally embraced this trend, even smaller businesses. It is a great time to leverage this trend; as a business, it creates a different level of conversation with a business partner. It enables you to be more differentiated and showcase the efforts you are making to your customers and distributors. As a supplier, you are intrinsically part of your customers' environmental balance. Your contribution can be positive or negative – why not make it positive?

Europeans have higher expectations than any other place on the planet when it comes to reducing their environmental impact, so it's crucial to take this into account. So while everyone else is thinking *it's all too hard*, imagine if you took advantage of these opportunities and context. Imagine how your business would look if you managed to generate your first million euros in sales in the next two years! What would your business look like?

OPPORTUNITIES IN THE EUROPEAN AGRICULTURAL TECHNOLOGIES SPACE

The Union has formulated very ambitious targets to modernize its agriculture. The Union has set several initiatives that plan to transform European agriculture into greener, safer, more modern, more connected agriculture.

Farm to Fork is one of the main initiatives to reduce the use of pesticides, reduce nutrient losses and use of fertilisers, and to further develop organic farming and reduce use of antimicrobials.[43] The Commission is taking actions to: reduce by 50% the use and risk of chemical pesticides by 2030; reduce by 50% the use of more hazardous pesticides by 2030; and to reach 25% of total farmland under organic farming by 2030.

The other interesting aspect is the digitization of farms, which includes **artificial intelligence (AI)**, **robotics**, the **internet of things (IoT)** and **5G**.[44] These are the areas identified by the EU to focus on to support

---

43 food.ec.europa.eu/horizontal-topics/farm-fork-strategy_en.
44 digital-strategy.ec.europa.eu/en/policies/digitalisation-agriculture.

European farmers and agribusinesses. It also goes down the value chain, using digitization to create a more streamlined value chain, with closer collaboration and improved communication between producers, processors, distributors, and retailers.

OPPORTUNITIES IN THE HEALTH TECHNOLOGIES

The last industry I would like to mention is the health, life science and pharma industry. The Union has planned a budget of €5.3 billion to promote and subsidize this area through its EU4Health grant program.[45] The main priority of the Union at the moment is to create a European Union of Health. Some of the priorities of the Union come from the lessons learnt from COVID, where coordination among members to provide emergency care for its population was lacking. It has defined as priorities to improve cross-border communication to fight health threats, and working on being better prepared by improving access and affordability to medicinal and other crisis-related products.

An initiative interesting for exporters is the digital transformation of healthcare, with better access to health data. Another major initiative to note is Europe's Beating Cancer, whose priorities include to improve cancer prevention, better support early diagnosis, have more personalized care, and better support patients with cancer.[46]

The European Union sees its pharmaceutical industry as a strategic asset to be able to provide highly skilled jobs and innovation. Taking on board the lessons from the past pandemic, the goal is to make sure that all Europeans have access to innovative therapies, with no shortages. For this to happen the Union needs to enhance its

---

45 hadea.ec.europa.eu/programmes/eu4health/about_en.
46 Europe's Beating Cancer Plan, Communication to the European Parliament and Council.

manufacturing capabilities and innovation abilities. This is what the EU Pharmaceutical Strategy is about.[47]

All these initiatives create a strong drive for companies in the med tech space to respond to immediate needs.

* * *

In summary, Europe offers a large range of opportunities for non-European companies entering the market, particularly in technology sectors: in AI & Digitization, Advanced Manufacturing, Robotics & Automation, Sustainability & Renewable, Agriculture & Food tech, as well as Health & Pharma.

Is It Time to Start Exporting to Europe?

---

47 health.ec.europa.eu/medicinal-products/pharmaceutical-strategy-europe_en.

Part II

Our export stories

Now the fun starts. I would like to introduce you to the companies we are going to examine. They are a diverse bunch, but they have several characteristics in common. Firstly, they are all active in the European market and their headquarters are located outside the European Union. Secondly, they are all selling to businesses and not to consumers. Most of these businesses are technology-based. You will read much more about them throughout the remainder of this book.

Chapter 3

Meet the companies

WHY THESE COMPANIES?

I decided to focus on small-, medium- and high-growth companies, who either are already established in the European market or are in the process of entering the market. They all have valuable insights to share. To give the journey some kind of homogeneity, I decided to mostly focus on businesses that develop a technology or a service that is technical, whether they are software developers, manufacturers or professional service providers. They all work in a business-to-business environment.

In my quest to collect stories of exporters to the European market, I made a point to have a diverse and rich perspective on Europe. That is why I interviewed a diverse range of nationalities. I share with you the perspectives of US, Australian, Japanese and Indian companies. My ambition with this choice of companies was to make the book as approachable as possible: wherever your business comes from, I hope you can find an insight that can be useful for your current European expansion.

We also have a mix of entry strategies, and the level of maturity of the businesses is quite diverse. All these perspectives bring a very interesting take on best practices for businesses to enter the European market.

What was also key in my quest was to talk to the professionals who actually worked on this European market entry project. It means that the interviewees, whether they are CEOs or executives, have firsthand experience on this market entry. They have done it themselves, usually with a team.

I decided to limit my interviews to only one of our Exportia customers. I focused on companies that don't work with my business to bring a fresh and unbiased perspective to you; also a great way for me not to lose an opportunity to keep learning.

A word of caution: The interviewees mostly speak under their own name, and their views do not always reflect the views of their businesses. It's important to understand that these stories happened in the past and do not disclose any information that could reflect their current market position.

Let me introduce you . . .

Bean Ninjas (Australia): the entry strategy of a service business

One of the major reasons I scouted Bean Ninjas is that they are an innovative service business. I am a strong believer in the fact that a lot of innovations and improvements in a business come from the act of looking at how different industries operate, learning from it and sometimes seeing how you can apply their best practices to a specific issue you are trying to solve. That is why the Bean Ninjas model and how they operate in Europe is interesting for any business, and particularly if you are a manufacturer or a cloud-based software business.

Headquarters	Australia, Gold Coast
Industry	Accounting and finance
Activity	E-commerce accountants
Size	11–50 employees
Company stage	Fast-growth small to medium enterprise
European position	Partner in the UK established in 2020 Project delivery team in Serbia
Who is talking to us	Tom Mercer, UK partner

E-commerce accountants and specialized services

The two founders, Meryl Johnston and Ben McAdam, started the business after reading *The 7 Day Startup* by Dan Norris. They got the business off the ground fairly quickly. The business was initially founded to provide bookkeeping services; it then started to focus on businesses specialized in e-commerce. The niche of Bean Ninjas is to offer best-in-class book-keeping, accounting, virtual CFO and tax services for seven- and eight-figure e-commerce businesses looking to scale. They have a unique positioning in this niche, given that traditional accounting firms, including the big four, do not know how to integrate multichannel transactions that are common practice in an e-commerce business. The other interesting side of this business is that from day one the business model was fully online and services were delivered by remote teams. Having built online communities, the business started to grow organically to the US, the UK, Hong Kong and Asia.

Person interviewed: Tom Mercer, Partner and Director, Bean Ninjas UK

Tom joined the business in January 2016, initially attracted by the ability the business provided to work from anywhere. He initially worked to support Bean Ninjas customers in the US and the UK, and is now focusing exclusively on growing the European market with his team.

Milestones

July 2015	Meryl Johnston and Ben McAdam launch Bean Ninjas with $1000 and a dream of changing the global bookkeeping game.
Dec. 2016	Bean Ninjas' growth journey continues with Meryl as solo Founder.
Dec. 2017	Bean Ninjas raises capital to fund rapid growth with private investor.
June 2019	Bean Ninjas enters the US market.
Feb. 2020	The world is hit with a pandemic, and this creates an opportunity for Bean Ninjas to become accounting leaders in e-commerce.
Sept. 2020	Bean Ninjas expands into Europe with Tom Mercer as Partner and Director.

CleanSpace Technology (Australia): the typical enterprise selling model

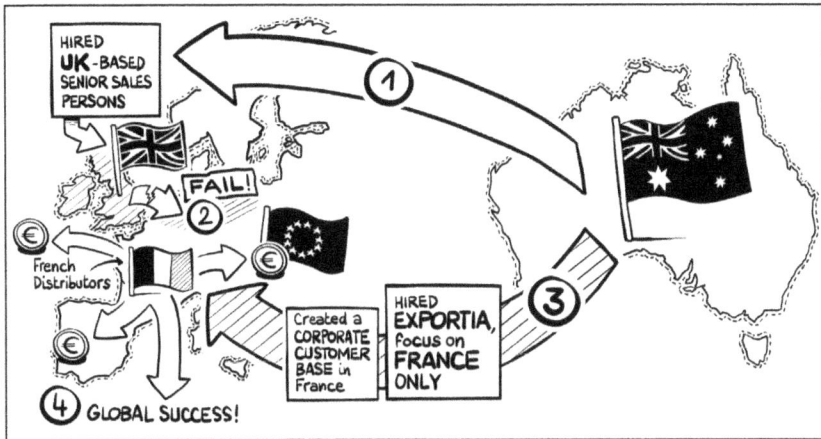

I chose to introduce you to CleanSpace because it has been one of our long-standing clients at Exportia. My team and I have had the pleasure of working with CleanSpace for close to 10 years. We have actively contributed and worked with their team to take their business to where they are now. This is a story of success. CleanSpace succeeded quickly in Europe, in my view because they embraced European diversity. We have not had to explain to them the value of translations and about bridging the gap with European customers – they understood it from day one.

Headquarters	Australia, Sydney
Industry	Safety devices
Activity	Manufacturing of powered-air purifying respirators
Size	101–250
Company stage	Listed on the Australian Securities Exchange (ASX: CSX)
European position	Europe-wide sales team and distributor network
Who is talking to us	Dr Alexandra Birrell, CEO *Alex has left CleanSpace and was CEO at the time of the interview.*

Respiratory protection devices for workers across industry and healthcare

CleanSpace specializes in the design, manufacturing and distribution of a unique and next-generation respiratory protection solution. The business operates in over 135 countries around the world, but principally works in more sophisticated markets, being the North America and the European markets.

It was founded in 2010 by a group of biomedical engineers. Dr Alex Birrell became the CEO in 2014.

The CleanSpace range of respirators protects workers across the globe against respiratory hazards (dust, gas, viruses) in very broad industry and healthcare applications.

The CEO of CleanSpace mentioned how new businesses, particularly new technology businesses, go through different stages. The first one tends to gravitate around the product and making sure that the product, design and support are fit for purpose, which requires getting a lot of customer feedback and validation. Once this has been done, it's time to grow sales.

From the management perspective, the focus starts to shift away from the product and more into the markets and the ability to supply that product. Most importantly, it's then critical to grow a customer base and to look at new markets as well as the sustainability of growth in existing markets.

Over the last six to seven years, the business has been really focused on its position in these markets, and its ability to grow and support broader adoption in these overseas markets.

The CleanSpace founders were engineers who brought their medical device experience into the industrial safety market, and brought a disruptive innovation to a market that had hardly seen any innovation in 20 years.

Person interviewed: Dr Alex Birrell, CEO

Dr Birrell has a dual background from her experience in hospitals and in the corporate sector, specifically in financial services at Pricewater-houseCoopers. So she brought her mix of technical and commercial skills to the business. She was instrumental at the time of raising funds and bringing shareholders on board, having a strong corporate background and view on the business.

Milestones

Five major milestones over a 10-year period in their successful market entry to Europe were:

- **Regulatory approval.** The home market of Australia was a good starting point, as it has a very good reputation for workplace safety. The Australian mining and construction sectors provided a nice precedent to grow the business internationally. However, Australia is relatively small compared to other markets. So, rapidly, it became really important to look at both Europe and North America. For CleanSpace, being in the safety industry, the regulatory approvals are real drivers. So once their first product was approved in Australia, it was the engineers who drove the market entry to Europe by obtaining the required certification. At the time, the decision was to prioritize Europe, as the regulatory process and partners made it quite transparent and easy to navigate and work through the regulatory process.

  The CEO mentions that at the initial stages of the business, the European market helped to shape their product design. So it was quite an important market for CleanSpace.

- **Entry to Europe.** At the time when the business looked at Europe, there were between 20 and 30 employees. The business at the time of the interview was over 100 employees.

- **Securing a partner to work on the European entry.** As they could not replicate in Europe the level of sales and technical support they have in Australia for the European market, it was critical to secure partners and distributors to be able to demonstrate the product and support the sales process technically.

- **A major European distributor coming on board.** A major milestone for Europe, when the brand and the technology were unknown, was to secure a major European distribution partner.

- **Signing large key accounts.** Distribution doesn't necessarily mean sales, so the next major milestone was getting some large key accounts on board and adopting the technology in Europe. That generated some major sales.

Du-Co Ceramics (US): gaining an international footprint via acquisition

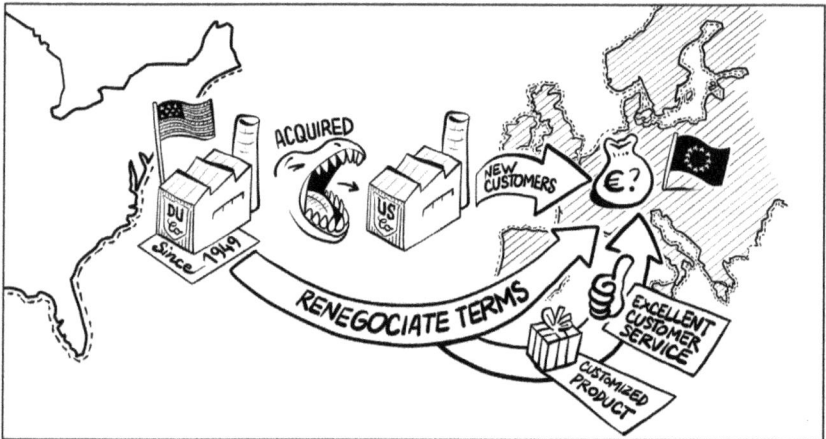

One of the interesting aspects in having Du-Co in the panel of interviews is the fact that they are a long-established business. They were founded in 1949! The other interesting aspect is the way they increased their market presence in international markets, including Europe, was through acquisition. It's another way to enter the European market.

They currently have a defined need for their product, which is quite mature in its life cycle. It means that customers can find them easily based on given specifications for most of their products. As they are a volume business they are in a price-sensitive market, and they have streamlined their processes to be able to compete.

They deal directly with end-users, and have no distribution partners. They can customize their products: same material, same process, different tooling. The same business model applies for the US and for Europe.

Headquarters	US, Saxonburg, Pennsylvania
Industry	Manufacturer of technical ceramics
Activity	Ceramics for ignition, heating industries
Size	250 staff
Company stage	Mature business Founded in 1949
European position	No team in Europe Direct contact with end-users, no distribution Acquired new European customers through acquisition
Who is talking to us	Tom Arbanas, President

The Du-Co Ceramics headquarters is in Saxonburg, Pennsylvania, US, near Pittsburgh. Du-Co employs 250 staff and is a fully integrated ceramics manufacturer. They have two manufacturing plants: one in Pennsylvania and one in North Carolina. They shop around the world. The business was founded in 1949, where the headquarters is currently located. Two gentlemen founded this company: Mr John J. Duke and Mr Reldon W. Cooper. Duke and Cooper decided on the name Du-Co, and then in the 1980s Mr Duke passed away and Mr Cooper's family became the sole owner of the company.

They are a high-volume manufacturer of technical ceramic components. They ship about a million parts a day directly from their facilities. They manufacture many different types of ceramic materials, including magnesium oxide, alumina ceramic, aluminum oxide, steatite ceramic, cordierite ceramic and forsterite ceramic. They use several manufacturing processes. They dry press ceramics, they extrude ceramics and roll compact ceramic materials.

Their ceramic products are often custom-designed and are used for a wide range of applications, including electric heat industries. They sell millions of ceramic rods and tubes to the resistor market. The third market they cater for is ignition applications for different types of gas ignition systems. Their ceramic parts are also used in a few unique applications, such as thermal sensors used in the Hubble telescope orbiting the planet, and in sonars for submarines. And a new application that recently emerged is ceramic with silver ions to filter water.

Person interviewed: Tom Arbanas, President of Du-Co

Tom's journey started at Pennsylvania State University, where he graduated with a ceramics science and engineering degree. He then worked for about five years at a ceramics manufacturing company in Latrobe, Pennsylvania. Then he had an opportunity to join Du-Co, and he has been there for almost 30 years. He started as a supervisor on the plant floor. He then became the Quality Manager for a few years. He then changed to Vice President of Sales, then became Vice President of Engineering. From there he became Vice President of Sales and Engineering. Finally, as Tom humorously describes it, as they could not find anything he could do right, they promoted him to President.

Milestones

1949	Business founded.
1980	Mr Duke passes away and the Cooper family becomes sole owner of the business.
2007	Acquisition of Saxon Ceramics, one of their competitors, which was going out of business.

The acquisition

Du-Co was already an exporter of a very small percentage of product to Europe, as well as Asia and Australia. Saxon did quite a bit more exporting, specifically to Europe. With the acquisition, Du-Co inherited these European customers. That prompted them to explore more of the European market.

Saxon Ceramics was a direct competitor. The two Du-Co founders had worked for the company, which was founded around 1911, before they left and founded Du-Co in 1949. Saxon had a different niche to Du-Co, and so the rationale behind the purchase was to increase the Du-Co customer base. Their core product fell right in line with Du-Co's core competencies, so they felt it would be a great acquisition. As they did complement Du-Co quite well, there was not a lot of extra equipment they would have to buy to integrate their product lines. The two businesses were located in the same city and lot of staff stayed on and worked for Du-Co. This really helped to keep good knowledge in the businesses.

Where they are now

'It seems to be over the past I'd say a couple of years, we seem to be gaining a larger footprint in Europe and we're not exactly sure why,' says Tom. However, the main work they have done is on upgrading their website, and they are seeing more traffic from it. He also thinks it might be due to the euro versus the dollar. The euro being stronger may have helped them to export more product to Europe.

Fluxergy (US): the start-up backed up by a billionaire

Fluxergy is an unusual start-up. At the time of the interview, it received approximately $50 million in funding from billionaire John Tu. The business provides a unique multimodal point-of-care system. Fluxergy has its own manufacturing. These are some of the quite unusual attributes for a start-up company. With strong financial backing and manufacturing already established, it is in a strong position to succeed in Europe.

Some of the interesting angles provided by this interview were due to the corporate background of Dr Tinazli. As a corporate veteran, he did not anticipate the effort it would take to get access to large European corporates as a new start-up, without a corporate domain name on his email address.

Headquarters	US
Industry	Laboratory technology
Activity	Multimodal detection technologies for laboratories
Size	43 employees at the time of the interview
Company stage	Start-up
European position	Pre-commercialization stage Pre-regulatory approval stage
Who is talking to us	Dr Ali Tinazli, Chief Commercial Officer

Two of the Fluxergy co-founders, Tej Patel and Ryan Revilla, are engineers who had experience in aerospace and Formula 1, so they were used to thinking about how they could fit as many detection systems and sensors as possible in a very small space. This is how their innovation for the laboratory market came about. Then they added the semiconductor industry perspective, where it's all about affordability and accessibility. This is how this disruptive technology is geared to scale to more people, as it becomes more affordable. And this is the perspective brought to the business from the semiconductor industry by John Tu, CEO of Kingston Technology Corporation and major shareholder of Fluxergy at the time of the interview.

Person interviewed: Dr Ali Tinazli, Chief Commercial Officer

Dr Tinazli joined Fluxergy when he lived in the US. He then went back to Germany to keep expanding the business towards Europe and Asia. He studied biochemistry and obtained a PhD in deeper studies of biophysics. He joined Applied Biosystems (which is Thermo Fisher now), where he was part of the corporate development team and was involved in technology scouting and technology licensing. He was then approached by Sony to join them. The objective was to build for Sony a new business in life sciences. He joined Sony in 2008, and was one of seven employees at Sony who started this new business. The business grew to 120 employees. That is when he decided to move back to the US, and he established an office for Sony in Cambridge, Massachusetts. Following this he was approached by HP, which intended to enter healthcare and hire Dr Tinazli to lead their global healthcare strategy out of the HP CTO office in Palo Alto. This strategy had been approved by the HP board, and that is when Dr Tinazli was approached by Fluxergy to join as a Chief Commercial Officer. He was convinced to join due to the unusual and attractive profile of this start-up.

Milestones

The business went very rapidly from 20 to 43 persons. Dr Tinazli said that the technology was ready for commercialization in 2020, due to numerous clinical studies with respected partners like the University of California San Diego and with Mass General Brigham. They worked with very well known top hospitals to prove technology readiness. Overall a great response was obtained from the evaluation period and the trials. In March 2021, Fluxergy was in pre-commercialization stage in Europe and Australia. The CE-IVD approval was obtained in Europe in March 2021 (two weeks after the interview). Dr Tinazli decided to move on from Fluxergy shortly after.

Futramed (US): looking at Europe, before venturing into their domestic market

The example of Futramed is interesting, as the founders made the decision to focus on the European market first before they would commercialize the technology in their home market, the US. This is why (at the time of writing) their product is approved in the European market and not in the US. The approach of Doug and Matt Harding to key opinion leaders in Europe is interesting. I especially thought that Matt's personable approach to business was worth sharing for non-Europeans. As a European myself, I thought Matt really was right in his approach there.

Headquarters	US, Utah
Industry	Medical devices
Activity	Hand-held medical device to treat chronic pain with the overall aim to reduce the use of opiate drugs.
Size	Micro-business
Company Stage	Pre-commercialization stage
European position	In the trial phase
Who is talking to us	Matt Harding, Vice President, International Son of founder Doug Harding

Person interviewed: Matt Harding, Vice President, International
Matt Harding is the Vice President, International of Futramed. Futramed is a US-based medical device company. Its head office is in Utah. Futramed was founded by Doug Harding, the father of Matt.

Futramed has patented a hand-held medical device to treat chronic pain. The overall mission of the business is to reduce opiate addiction and overdose resulting from prescription drugs, which is a major healthcare challenge globally.

The hand-held, battery-powered device was developed by Doug. He met French physician Aimé Limoge in the early 2000s through a mutual business connection. The physician created a waveform that was called the Limoge current. Transcutaneous cranial electrical stimulation with Limoge current has been proven to facilitate anesthesia/analgesia in surgical patients. In simple words, when the current is delivered to the patient with the right electrode montage, it has the potential of creating opioids and thus reduces pain.

The French physician had built at the time a very large device to be able to conduct his studies. He asked Doug if he could engineer a modernized and more compact device that would enable the commercialization of the invention in a medical device. Doug developed a small handheld battery-powered version of the Limoge current with some components that are patented. This is what formed the basis of Futramed. Aimé Limoge passed away in 2010.

Futramed is at the pre-commercialization and fundraising stage. They don't consider themselves as strong in the export game. They rather have felt their way through exports as Matt Harding was in Spain.

Milestones

2000	Meeting between Doug Harding and Aimé Limoge
2012	Matt joins the business, moving to Spain to set up European operations. This is when he starts to interface with local key opinion leaders in the medical sector. His motivation is based on meeting Dr Luis Stinus, one of Aimé Limoge's colleagues who worked extensively on Limoge current and contributed to the early development of the device.
2020	CE approval
2022	Fundraising for the development of the manufacturing capabilities of the device. Soft launch in France through initial trials currently being conducted (at the time of writing).

Joe L. (US), Vice President: plugging into existing European ecosystems to grow software sales

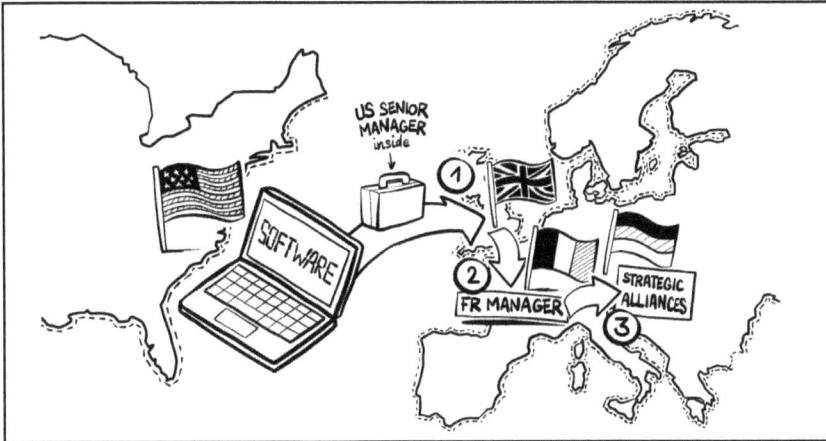

The business has been around for about 20 years. It was founded by some university professors just trying to find mathematical applications within business. Initially, it involved a lot of typical consulting work and it then became artificial intelligence. No one called it this at the time. And in the B2B business world it has only become significant and meaningful in the past three to four years. So a lot of what the business was doing at the time was then categorized as data science. The business helps enterprise-size B2B organizations with optimizing their sales use cases.

The European market is strategic for this software business. Their technology is cutting edge. Typically when it comes to software, the US adopts first, then certain countries in Europe and then the rest of Europe.

I found the interview with Joe extremely interesting, as he honestly shared some of the early learnings the business had to go through. He notably explains why a channel partner strategy should have been adopted earlier. The other fascinating aspect of the interview is how he emphasizes the importance of the right European country selection to make sure to cover your total addressable market, hence for them they should probably have chosen to start with Germany from day one in Europe. He also talks about the pivotal moment when they started to achieve very ambitious goals in Europe.

These talking points are very interesting for businesses not only in the software game, but also for any business targeting large multinationals as their customers and looking at forming or resetting their entry strategy into the European market.

Headquarters	US
Industry	Cloud-based software
Activity	Pricing and sales software for B2B environment
Size	Medium-sized business
Company stage	20 years in business
European position	Offices in London, Paris and Germany
Who is talking to us	Joe L. is the Vice-President, Global Partners & Alliances

Milestones

The business started primarily in the US. They started to sell to large companies, and from within each of the large corporates they worked with they started to expand into other business units. This means that in some cases they sold to business units headquartered in Europe. They would staff these operations with Americans initially to implement the projects. It wasn't until they had some level of success that they decided to hire somebody local in sales. And so after a while they started to have salespersons in addition to sending team members for project implementations. And it all grew from there.

1	The first hire in Europe was an American General Manager sent to Europe, who knew the product well.
2	The business had been 10 years in Europe when they really started investing. When they started to look at the total addressable market in Europe is when they really started to drive European expansion.
3	The business now focuses on the US and Europe, and is responding to demands from other regions on an opportunistic basis.
4	The business has offices in London, Paris and Germany. They have a very small office in Milan. They have 35% of their employees in Europe on the service side, and 40% of the sales team is in Europe.

Phoenix Medical Systems (India): using what the European market needs as a benchmark to embrace manufacturing excellence and continuous improvement

Phoenix Medical Systems is a 30-year-old company specializing in the manufacture of infant and maternal care medical equipment. It started in 1989, when India did not have any manufacturing of this kind of equipment. It was all imported into India, and so it was expensive. The spares were expensive too, and it was hard to get any service support and doctors found it quite difficult to take care of babies and newborns.

That is why the current director of Phoenix, who is a graduate of the prestigious Indian Institute of Technology, made his university project to make a prototype of a baby incubator. He then placed it in a maternity hospital. The doctors' enthusiasm triggered him to create an enterprise. The doctors decided to support the enterprise with the clear vision to end suffering, given the price of the imported technologies from Europe and the US. The business started very small, and is now the largest manufacturer in India. They have three factories.

The director wanted to see the technology commercialized overseas; he had this ambition early on. One of the drivers was to counterbalance the fact that this type of product was only sold by large players such as GE, Dräger and Siemens. The lower- and middle-income countries could not afford this kind of equipment. So the director started to look for a person to take care of international markets, and that is when Vinod started. Vinod has been enjoying working for the company for the last 17 years. When he started there was absolutely zero exports.

When you are an Indian company, overseas markets drive better profit margins and better payment terms, so there is a lot of appeal to going overseas. The decision to look at the European market was incidental. Basically in the medical device sector, the entire world converges towards Germany. People in this sector from all around the world go to the Medica trade fair, so the decision was made to display the product there and that is how the first connections were made.

The experience of Phoenix Medical with the European market is one of a search for continuous improvement and excellence. Even though the European market is not a direct export market for Phoenix, it is a strategic one for the business. Key non-governmental organizations have their headquarters in Europe, and Phoenix has had to seek their endorsements to be well positioned to sell the Phoenix technology to a diverse range of countries with low purchasing power. This quest has resulted in Phoenix taking a hard and honest look at the way they did things at the time and at introducing major improvements in their business to match European standards, needs and expectations.

Headquarters	India
Industry	Medical devices
Activity	Infant and maternal care medical equipment
Size	Small to medium
Company stage	Founded in 1989 Mature business well established in its domestic market Three production sites Exports to 60 countries
European position	Key strategic partnerships in place in Europe to access key Europe-headquartered NGOs No staff in Europe
Who is talking to us	Vinod Narayanan, CEO Africa and Americas

Meet the companies

Person interviewed: Vinod Narayanan, CEO Africa and Americas

Vinod came into the company in 2004. At the time, Phoenix was only a domestic player. When Vinod came in, he started the export department as a single person. He was doing everything from sales to export documentation to logistics. He loves the maternity field. His previous job was with MRF in tyre manufacturing, where he worked as a senior export marketing officer. This was a very large organization, which made Vinod feel only a very small part of a very large company. So when he joined Phoenix, he loved the challenge of starting exports from zero. Today Phoenix exports to 60 countries.

Milestones

1989	Company founded
2004	Phoenix exhibits at Medica for the first time First meeting with Swiss company Initial interest from Eastern European countries
2008	CE certificates received for several products Strike OEM manufacturing deal for Swiss business

Vigience (Japan): two attempts to enter Europe and how the second much leaner approach resulted in success.

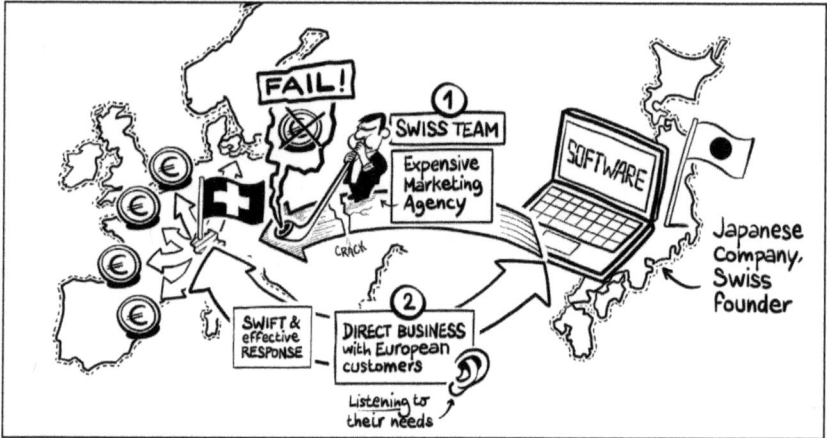

Vigience connects Salesforce CRM with the SAP platform. If a customer is using a CRM like Salesforce they cannot see if they can ship a product next week, and they cannot see a customer-specific price or discount, making it quite hard to process an order. With the Vigience product, Overcast, they can easily access all this information.

Vigience was founded in Japan by Markus Stierli. It now has 25 employees. The business has located its headquarters in the US with the objective of having a foot in Silicon Valley. But their development team and most of their employees are based in Japan. They also have a few employees in Europe. It was initially founded as a software consulting firm and Markus Stierli, the founder, made the decision to transform it into a full software company about 10 years ago.

Fukushima, which was quite a disaster for Japan, accelerated the process of looking at international markets, with the company being unsure how stable the Japanese economy would be. In addition, a couple of the Vigience staff who were Europeans decided to go back to Europe. That was another trigger. In retrospect, Markus thinks this triggered them to go to the US and Europe a bit earlier than they would otherwise have gone. They also thought that they would get early adopters from the European market. And it would help them to trigger more references in their home market in Japan, where references are extremely important.

Markus pictures in this interview the best lesson any exporter can learn. He demonstrates how a successful entry to the European market may take several attempts. He also shows how setting up a European office and conducting the typical marketing campaign did not work for them. He shares with us what drove their success the second time. I find his message powerful and full of hope for SMEs: you just need to win one customer at a time and fully understand their needs to succeed. As simple as that!

The key message for Japanese companies is interesting too. In Japan, access to large corporates is often done through partners. However, Markus's business would not have direct contact with the large Japanese corporates. It is the opposite in Europe – trust is built directly with large corporates before a business can build the channel eco-system to support the large corporate.

Headquarters	Japan, Tokyo
Industry	Software
Activity	Connector between Salesforce and SAP
Size	SME, 25 employees
Company stage	Founded in 2006 High-growth SME
European position	A few employees in Europe
Who is talking to us	Markus Stierli, CEO and Founder

Person interviewed: Markus Stierli, CEO and Founder

Markus Stierli is a German-speaking Swiss national. He worked for SAP for about 12 years and had the pleasure of building up the SAP development center in Japan. After about 12 years, he started his own company, first as an SAP consultancy and they are now an independent software vendor.

Milestones

2010	Business founded by Markus Stierli
2011	First attempt to go to Europe, triggered by the Fukushima disaster Creation of an entity in Switzerland Relocation of a small team of European employees to Switzerland
2019–20	Complete change of strategy for the European market A more direct approach to end-users, large corporates

Chapter 4

About the interviews

Now that I have introduced the companies to you, I am going to take a brief step back and outline for you how I went about interviewing these companies and how they entered the European market. In my business, we use a simple 7 Pillar model.

Each of the companies responded to my questions through the prism of the 7 Pillars. And I have used this model to present to you these entry strategies. There is a lot to learn from each of these approaches for any business going to Europe. Here are the 7 Pillars we use in my business when we work with small-, medium- and high-growth businesses in Europe.

Pillar 1: Product		Proven Compliant Protected Positioned

In terms of guidelines, I usually give the following recommendations to our customers as they enter the European market. Their product must be **proven**, as in it must have a track record as a minimum in their domestic market. They must **comply** with European standards as a minimum. They also must have **protected** their intellectual property – even though the European market is generally quite respectful, you also need to be clear that you are not infringing on anyone's IP. The product or solution must also have a clear **positioning** in comparison to major competitors, particularly European ones, without forgetting indirect competition.

For the product pillar, what I was interested to hear from the interviewees is why Europeans liked their products or software and bought it. I wanted to know if they had to make any specific changes to their product to satisfy the needs of their European customers, or if in the end European customers just had the same needs as their domestic market.

So the interviewees were asked the following three questions:

- Why do you think your product has been successful in Europe?

- What do you think Europeans loved about your product?

- Did you have to adapt your product for Europe?

Pillar 2: Customers		Focus on one or two customer profiles that you have a proven track record with.

When entering the European market, focusing on the customer profile you know best is one of the general recommendations we provide to our customers. The other advice is to be initially very focused in one specific profile of customer. It means being focused on a specific industry (for example, hospitals), or on a certain typology of client (large multinationals with a turnover > €500 million).

An important aspect when approaching a European customer is to know what problem the product or solution is solving for this customer in this industry. Traction with European leads and customers is usually obtained when the company really knows the issues their customers are facing and when they are able to demonstrate how they solve these issues and that they have done it before, and even better have a track record doing it with faster results in Europe.

For these interviews, I asked the companies which customers they focused on. But the most interesting part I really wanted to know was how they went about identifying and signing up their first European customers. I think there's always value in looking at different industries and companies and learning how they went about it. I also was interested to know if they had encountered any challenges not being a European business.

Here are the questions I asked them, but of course in many cases, and to my delight, the conversations went much broader:

- How did you identify and secure your first European customers?

- Were there challenges not being a European business? (Time difference, European competitors, etc.)

About the interviews

Pillar 3: Country		Conduct a sound country selection – focus on one or two countries maximum to start with.

Conducting a country selection process sounds basic, but it is actually really important to avoid any delay in creating traction in Europe. **It is easier to create traction in a smaller geographical area, where you can create a snowball effect faster.** It is quite costly and takes more time to generate revenue in multiple countries at the same time. That is why it is important to choose the right country to focus on. The choice has to be twofold: the market size of course, and at the same time the appetite of the market. Germany is the largest European market in many industries, but is it the market where buyers are going to buy your product in the short to medium term? This needs to be part of the assessment. In some instances, it can be quite a long process and may come easier in another market that is smaller.

For these reasons, I was really interested to hear how the interviewees went about it.

Here are some of the questions I asked:

- What made you decide to export to Europe?

- How did you select which country to focus on in Europe?

- Did you start with any country in particular? Why?

- Were you more successful in a specific country in comparison to another one? Why?

- How did you find Europe in comparison to the US market?

- Did you find any country harder to enter in in comparison to other countries?

Pillar 4: Sales channels, distributors		Profile, select, engage, activate and manage sales channels to reach your European sales target.

Sales channels, otherwise called distributor or channel partners, are a very useful tool for small and medium-sized companies entering Europe. It gives them the reach to a large number of customers; it expands their territory coverage. A European distributor may have a salesforce of hundreds of representatives presenting your product. And it is one of the classic ways of generating sales without the risk of hiring locally. The main process we take our customers through when setting up distributors in Europe is first to **profile** their ideal channel partners by using the characteristics that have been successfully working for them.[48] In the preselected countries, map out and **select** the channel partners that best match this profile. Then it's time to **engage** with them to assess if they are the right partner for your business and if you can come to a distribution agreement.

The most important phase starts now. It is time to **activate** the channel partner by training them, to work with selected sales champions within their organization, and to generate leads for them to be interested in selling your product. Basically this is how you can start generating revenue with a channel partner. To maintain this growth and development in revenue, it's then time to **manage** the distribution partner to make sure they keep performing according to plan.

When setting up with distributors, I always like to recommend our customers go non-exclusive. I find it too risky for small businesses to

---

48 This step-by-step distributor engagement process is detailed in my second book, *The Four Steps to Generate Your First Million Euros in Sales*, in chapter 4 about sales channels.

work exclusive arrangements. If the channel partner does not perform, it takes too long to unwind the relationship and to start again on a plan B. I also like to have a mix of profiles; very large players give you the reach but small and agile players give you the speed a small-, medium- and high-growth business needs.

For these reasons, I was very intrigued to learn from the interviewees about their experience with European distribution partners. I really wanted to share with you how they went about it.

Here are some of the questions I asked:

- Are you working with European distributors? How did you select your European distributors?

- How do you work with your European distributors? How do you get them motivated?

- If you were to set up distribution in Europe now, what would you do differently?

Pillar 5: Marketing		A sharp value proposition tailored to your ideal customer profile is a good preliminary step to any lead-generation campaign.

In our small-, medium- and high-growth companies world, we mainly focus on marketing that generates leads. Otherwise, what's the point? This category usually has limited funds for marketing, so it's better to have a good return on marketing dollars. So, **laser focus is again key**. First, developing a clear, consistent and high-impact value proposition that can be used throughout your marketing is important. Then formalize customer references, in the form of testimonials and case studies, that can be used to demonstrate you are a credible player in the market. Identify trade shows, conferences or events that your ideal customer profiles are actively participating in. Attend digitally or in person to present and to exhibit; doing both at the same time will have the best payoff. Shows are a good basis to start a lead-generation campaign. There are other ways to generate lists of customer targets, but if you do not have a local expert helping you navigate the local market, shows are a great way to start. Our experience is that online and social media campaigns when you just start in European are quite inefficient, as you do not have enough knowledge of the market to finetune them and make them efficient.

So again, I was very intrigued to see what the interviewees did in terms of marketing. What worked and what did not work? It's easy to spend a lot of marketing dollars on inefficient marketing, so it's always better to learn from others! Here are some of the questions I asked the interviewees:

- In terms of marketing, what worked well to create awareness about your product in Europe?

- Did you have to alter your approach to your marketing in Europe? In what way?

- How was it a different strategy to your home market?

- What specific activities worked well (campaigns, shows, conferences, etc.)?

Pillar 6: Team		Get your entire team engaged in maximizing the export effort, being familiar with European customers and ready to give them the best support.

Small and medium-sized businesses and particularly high-growth businesses exporting are facing many challenges. One of the main ones is staffing and resourcing. It is typically hard for a high-growth business to make sure it has sufficient resources. It is always running with a small team. And export is one more task the team at the headquarters has to get started and grow, and sometimes remotely. It can be an inhibitor for the growth of exports.

When it comes to the teams that lead to export success, **getting your entire team engaged and trained to support the export effort is a key activity**. Then when the initial export leads and sales are more developed, it is time to start hiring in Europe. There are many challenges in this process – sometimes companies hire too soon, in the wrong country, or the wrong profile. It's hard to hire in a different country when you are unaware of the local diplomas and the different career paths. On top of these challenges, when you start in Europe, you don't always have networks. That is why I was interested to ask questions to see how these companies worked on this issue and navigated the HR challenges of recruiting in Europe.

Here are some of the questions I asked:

- At the initial stages, when you started in Europe, which persons in your business were involved in the process? How many persons? What were their roles in the company?

- Do you have a team in Europe?

- When did you start recruiting in Europe? What triggered the need to start having people based in Europe?

- What was your most successful recruitment? How did it happen? Why do you think it was the most successful?

- What piece of advice would you give to a company about to recruit their first salesperson in Europe?

Pillar 7: Dashboard		Tracking progress in the European markets like you would do in your own domestic market is important.

Essentially in this pillar we work with businesses on how they are going to track their export progress. It's not always an easy task; **when you start in a market you don't always know when you are going to start generating revenue**. Therefore, assigning a sales target too soon may not be relevant nor useful in any way. Instead, it may be more useful to have some simple objectives that can be quantified: getting feedback from 20 distributors within three months, or getting a trial with a large multinational in the next quarter. And that is a good way to track activities that can lead to reaching the KPI. We also find that small businesses don't always have tools to capture their progress, report back and keep track. I was of course curious to know how these companies are organized around this pillar, and if there is any conclusion to draw from their responses.

Here are two of the questions I asked:

- How did you track your progress in Europe?

- Did you establish any specific processes to manage your team in Europe?

Chapter 5

How each company approached the European market

THE 7 PILLAR APPROACH

This chapter gives you an insider view of how these businesses entered the European market. This is a rare opportunity that I am delighted to share with you.

I've highlighted the key points in each interview, to make it easier for you to learn from these them. Let's get started!

CleanSpace Technology: very strong relationships with their European target market at trade shows

'Europe is a big market. You have to know where to invest time and energy.'

1. Country initial focus: Decision on France

2. Customer focus (Construction) + Channels
(large distribution partners, strong focus on a small number of distributors + Marketing (show)

3. Team (recruit) to support growth

4. Expand to more markets

How each company approached the European market

Is It Time to Start Exporting to Europe?

European construction companies, particularly with large operations that had exposure to silica, silica dust and fibers. And that was really their first entry to Europe; they tried to apply what they learned in Australian and to replicate it in Europe.	Clearly differentiated and positioned a respiratory product range in comparison with the current products in the market.	CleanSpace initially tried a broad brush of markets and then landed in France.
There were challenges initially to set up teams, so they used trusted partners to support them, like Exportia. For fast-growth companies, you must have a team able to read what's coming up and adapt. Hire only once you know the market.	European industry shows are of very high quality and provide opportunities to connect to customers. For the CleanSpace CEO, the trade shows were one of the most effective ways to learn about the European market, if you compare it to some advertising or social media.	CleanSpace sees distribution as a partnership. The distributor and the supplier are working together to get sales and get the customer to adopt the solution. So it means that the distributor relationship and strategy always starts with a customer, the end-user for the product.
		CleanSpace's main focus is to measure activity driving sales. That's important in the early stages. Then of course sales and pipeline. Some of the indicators that are watched help ensure that the right type of customers are in the pipeline; for example, large corporations instead of small and medium-sized businesses and individuals. The business tracks the sales activity with CRM software, like most organizations.

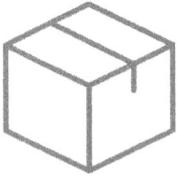

Product

'Europe shaped a lot of our designs.'

'Europeans genuinely saw the advantages of our solution, compared to those traditional models, so, something that would give them higher protection, was super easy to use and very comfortable so deployable across a large workforce, and it was cost effective and sustainable for the environment. A reusable system like CleanSpace offers lots of advantages for that and decreases a lot of waste.'

Dr Alex Birrell found that the company did not make any product adjustments specific to Europeans; she said that the strong European culture for safety and their sophisticated manufacturing and industry operations shaped the product. She even goes beyond and highlights that the CleanSpace team learnt a lot from the European market. It had a lot of input into their design pipeline; it made it more robust and far more advantageous and attractive globally.

As I mentioned earlier in the book, CleanSpace was a customer of my business Exportia and I worked very closely with them for close to 10 years. As I reflect on my work with CleanSpace, what was a clear accelerator was their ability to innovate in a market that had not innovated for 20 years. What I also found interesting was that the innovation came from a team of biomedical engineers who worked on respiratory in a healthcare application in their previous careers and so brought a fresh perspective on the industrial respiratory market, which had only incrementally innovated. Having introduced this innovation to several industries in Europe, notably in France and Germany, I can report that the product acceptance in these markets in the early stages has been phenomenal.

Customers

To enter into the European market, CleanSpace was trying to replicate their experience in their domestic market (Australia):

'We were looking for similar customers. Australia has a lot of mining customers, so we were looking at some of the European construction companies, particularly with large operations that had exposure to silica, silica dust and fibers. And that was really our first entry to Europe; we tried to apply what we learned in Australian and replicate it in Europe.'

In my experience, businesses that have a track record in a specific industry can enter the European market faster and reach success faster than others. European customers will always relate more to peers even if they are thousands of kilometers away. Mining companies and construction in this case were facing the same challenges for their workers. All the accumulated experience of CleanSpace in mining definitively was an accelerator in Europe.

Dr Birrell recognizes they were fortunate to have been able to do that. What was harder to replicate was the support – getting the sales support and technical support to these customers.

'We need to find new partners and new salespeople, to help us find the right support from distribution. Finding the right partners in order to introduce and demonstrate the product was really key for us in Europe.'

> Of course, businesses new to the European market won't be able to replicate straight away the same support as with its own team in a domestic market. At the start, the local team is not there yet. CleanSpace was smart to leverage its distribution partners to provide additional support.

Country
CleanSpace initially tried a broad brush of markets and then landed in France.

CleanSpace initially went out to a number of markets; they tried a lot of distribution partners and they tried to work across about eight markets. But ultimately they got traction in France.

'And that was really off the back of a couple of key things. One of them was our partner Exportia.' That is when they started to focus on market adoption and get sales growth. In that process about finding the right partners, CleanSpace was able to find three or four really strong partners for that market. And then we were able to build the market into different parts of France. That is really when it started.

Where sales really took off was when they had done their assessment and they realized that France was where they had the most traction and the market should receive all their attention to grow sales. I cannot reiterate enough how a focused approach on one country at a time has far more success than a broad 'shotgun' approach. For us at Exportia, it has always been critical to our customers' success. It seems to me that sometimes businesses new to Europe forget that exporting to a specific country means that it's as if they are starting a new business all over again. And that is why it deserves full focus and attention. It's not just a marginal addition to their business and something they can conduct on the side and see how they go. Focus is critical to success. This is something that CleanSpace understood and is one of the reasons why they got good traction in France.

Europe has been a very successful market for CleanSpace. Europe has a lot of large markets for CleanSpace but is still quite fragmented. CleanSpace has good reference sites, distribution partners and plenty of growth in these core large markets. CleanSpace is also now looking at other countries within Europe, with a similar set up. Some of the languages become a bit more difficult because you need to provide support in four or five languages. To support that, CleanSpace have been able to adapt and evolve into a multilingual team to be able to provide support across a number of countries. Brexit has created an additional complexity for a lot of companies. It has required Clean-Space to do a reset to support the UK as well as Europe.

Sales channels, distributors

Dr Birrell sees the first milestone that was critical to the business progressing as a major distribution partner coming on board. The CleanSpace team also experienced that distribution does not necessarily mean sales, so the second milestone was getting some large key accounts as customers. First sales are experimental and they are usually small; really entering the European market like it's your own backyard means getting a large reference site on board in a major way. That is what CleanSpace calls a 'large deployment'. Having a large distribution partner to validate the brand and having them support these large reference sites was important.

This point underlined by Dr Birrell is critical. Once the key target customers are identified (for them it was construction), as the business does not have the local support based in Europe instantly, this is when it's critical to appoint the distribution partners that are going to be able to sign these large corporate accounts and more importantly support them locally. These distribution partners often have contracts with large accounts. So as a newcomer to the market, particularly from far-away Australia, having a very large, well-established partner creates instant credibility with these large corporate customers. The exporters move from a status of an unknown entity, potentially risky, to a low-risk partner, just by having set up the right partner locally.

'CleanSpace found Germany to be more fragmented regionally in its distribution. There are more regional and local distributors and fewer big national distributors. To get volume you have to appoint many distributors, whereas France has nice big national distributors. It's easier to get in and across the market fairly quickly. Some markets are a little slower and more complex.'

This is where I find that it is so important to test a market. Typically Germany, on paper, often looks like the largest European market. In many different industries this is the case, given its population and solid industry base. But having tested several European markets, CleanSpace was able to determine that France offered rapid traction. And having targeted large multinationals as a key strategy made it easy for CleanSpace to become an attractive partner of a large distribution partner. Large corporate accounts rarely sign large corporate agreements with small distribution partners.

'You always need to add value to the distribution channel.'

'CleanSpace sees distribution as a partnership. Both the distributor and the supplier are working together to get sales and get the customer to adopt the solution. So it means that the distributor relationship and strategy always starts with a customer, the end-user for the product.

'The CleanSpace team makes a point to get that right. It means that you need to be prepared and do the work with the customer and then bring the lead back to the distributor.

'It means showing to the distributors that the product can be sold and showing them a picture of success. You have to keep doing that, because distributors can be quite large, with lots of reps. Some of the sales reps learn, and then they go to another distributor. It's never set. Then a new rep starts. It's a continuous process to help distributors build their business around your product. CleanSpace also finds it quite important to keep the distributors' sales team trained and knowledge-able about the product, because they have 10,000 products to sell. It's not fair to assume they are going to remember CleanSpace.'

> In my view, this is where many businesses entering the European market with distributors get it wrong. And this is where CleanSpace got it 100% right. Companies get it wrong when they sign distribution partners and wait for them to miraculously start selling. This is what makes a difference between success and failure. Distributor sales representatives often have a large portfolio of products to sell. For them to be comfortable selling a new technology, and we find this is true for any type of technology, the manufacturer needs to hold their hand through the initial stages, to take them to success.

'CleanSpace is a good product for distributors. It's a door opener and it makes them look good, as it makes their company look like they are bringing new technology to their customers. But we constantly need to be educating them and refreshing their product knowledge.

'CleanSpace made the decision not to establish too many distribution partners at the same time. This makes sure the company can invest in the distributor and the distributor invests in the partnership.'

> This last comment is particularly important for small and medium-size companies entering the European market. Having a clear map of distribution partners and doing a

thorough selection is important. We saw a lot of businesses come to us after having failed, when they had spread themselves thinly among too many different countries and ended up having to manage too many distributors and in too many countries at the start. As you can see with CleanSpace, one of the reasons they were able to create fast traction is that they focused their resources on getting one market right (France). And it was doubled by the fact that they also appointed only a limited number of distribution partners, and that they were able to put a lot of focus on at the start. It was a very successful strategy.

Team

> *'There were challenges initially to set up teams, so we used trusted partners to support us, like Exportia.'*

Seven or eight years back, the CEO of CleanSpace mentioned that the difficulty was to find people who understand your business at the initial stages of the process and not just some sort of on-the-ground salespeople, but actually people you could trust.

'Products being sold in a business-to-business environment are sold at the operations level, but you also need someone that can navigate the corporate decision-making process. If you are selling to corporates, you need to find someone who can do both. It requires getting the right people and being fairly swift in those conversations. That was the key for us in people. We did not do well in the beginning.

'I think one of the keys, and I've always said it with Exportia, is not only do you operate at that ground level to get the buy in to get the trials, to make sure it's successful. But also step into a corporate role to be able to navigate and negotiate through some of those larger corporate processes.

'For fast-growth companies it's about having a team able to read what's coming up and adapt. But the other thing I think we found with our partners is that – in particular Exportia – the ability to evolve with our business, and that was an absolute key. The business is dynamic, and particularly as a growth business, you need partners who can evolve with you. They can morph their skillset, but they can equally change their role over time. And it's not about doing less or more, it's about what the business needs to be successful and being able to be quite fluid and read what's coming up and be able to adapt accordingly, so it's much more of a forward-looking model than you know what we're doing now, because that will change.'

CleanSpace made the decision to hire an outsourced sales team like Exportia to get the sales started in Europe, particularly in France and then in other parts of Europe. I think the take away for any business here is that a business should really only hire once they have created some traction in the market. Non-European businesses tend to hire someone that they will then rely on to make it happen. In my business, Exportia, we have seen so many businesses hiring a salesperson in the wrong country opportunistically, via an acquaintance or a business connection, pre-Brexit the recruitee would be based in the UK. A UK-based person without the language skills required and the in-market knowledge will find it very difficult to enter the French or the German market. It is not how it works. This is what CleanSpace understood and made the decision to first generate revenue, know their market and then recruit a team to support their growth in the right country. I think in terms of speed of generating revenue that was extremely efficient.

'Not having a team there can make you miss out on opportunities.'

Dr Birrell goes on about some challenges that were highlighted – the fact that when a customer sends you an e-mail or gives you a call, they have your product in their head for five minutes and then they move on to something else.

'You have a very short window of opportunity to capture the lead and engage. That is the reason why you need people on the ground.'

On one hand, you need people on the ground to capture and work on these leads, but on the other hand it's hard to hire locally in Europe right at the start. At the start of your European journey, you don't know where your customers are going to be. You don't know which language you're going to get the most traction in, thus what languages your first hires will need to speak.

So you do need to spend some time in Europe and you need to invest in it as a business. You need to know the market and work out where you are going to get that traction from. It could be the Nordics, the UK, France, Germany or the Netherlands.

This is where you are going to get traction and you will be able to form some relationships that are going to help you find good people. This is where CleanSpace learnt from their original mistake. Before they hired Exportia, they hired in a market where they did not specifically have traction. Dr Birrel says they think they should have spent more time learning about that market themselves before that initial attempt to hire. Then, with Exportia they knew where to invest that time and energy.

Marketing

European industry shows are of very high quality to connect to customers. CleanSpace has found that these shows have been very effective.

Traditional print advertising and social media campaigns can still be done, but marketing in different languages adds complexity. However, the CleanSpace team found that at some of the industry shows, you don't necessarily need to speak the language. A lot of businesspeople can speak English, and if the product and the technology is really attractive, they will find a way to understand a little bit more. For the CleanSpace CEO, the trade shows were **one of the most effective ways to learn about the European market**, if you compare it to some advertising or social media.

CleanSpace replicated the same messages in Europe. 'Key messages were the same in Europe and in our domestic market in Australia. It comes back to the fact that Australia, our domestic market, has a very sophisticated and advanced workplace safety culture.'

This is also because regulatory frameworks around workplace safety are very similar in Europe and in Australia. Europe and Australia often have the same local bodies like WorkCover or WorkSafe, and CleanSpace were able to identify the same types of organizations in Europe. This was helpful to understand the market a bit more.

CleanSpace overall found a lot of parallels between Australia and Europe in their industry. It means that the key messages could stay the same.

Interestingly, CleanSpace, like several of the interviewees, have formed very strong relationships with their European target market at trade shows. Of course, this is a cost-effective way to connect with a lot of customers in one location, with the exhibitors and the visitors. With more than 20 years of presence on these European shows, I find that a lot of long-term business relationships materialize over the years at these shows. And often it's because once they have found 'their' industry show in Europe, companies invest in it. And Europeans take it as proof of a serious business, to have a stand at the given industry show year after year. It demonstrates stability. This is a key strategy in the marketing mix for any non-European business entering this market. And my recommendation is to step out of the region/country pavilion and have your own stand as soon as you can. These country/regional pavilions are cost effective and a great start. But to build your brand, have your own stand. CleanSpace always had a very professional stand from the early years and year after year it really built their brand.

Dashboard

The business tracks sales activity with CRM software, like most organizations.

CleanSpace's main focus is to measure activity driving sales. That's particularly important in the early stages in a new market like Europe. Then of course the pipeline of leads, opportunities and sales. Some of the indicators that are watched ensure that the right type of customer is in the pipeline; for example, large corporations instead of small and medium-size businesses and individuals. To achieve good conversion, the other indicator that is watched is the response times to leads. CleanSpace makes sure that leads are responded to in a timely manner. That is an important indicator captured in the CRM.

Fluxergy: a case of pre-commercialization: what can be done prior to compliance?

Fluxergy is an unusual start-up, as best described by Dr Tinazli. It's a fully funded start-up. This business illustrates quite well what companies can do prior to full compliance with European standards.

	What you can do without compliance*	What you can't do without compliance*
	Establish and prioritize the best European countries for your business	Sell your products
	Test your pricing	Get your distributors to hold stock while compliance is getting ready
	Assess the interest and requirements of European distributors	Free samples

* Each European directive will describe in detail what type of activity (trialing, providing samples, selling) are covered by the EU compliance. I find that a lot of businesses leave compliance to the last minute, whereas once you know which region will be your focus, compliance needs to happen as early as possible.

Is It Time to Start Exporting to Europe?

Two segments are being pursued:
- equine
- human health.

Two products are being pursued:
- COVID-19 PCR tests
- equine tests for horses.

Seeking compliance at the time of the interview limited the ability to work aggressively on commercialization.

Focus on the German market to capitalize on the expertise of the senior team.

Initially: Eastern Europe, as they have a high rate of new labs, which opens more opportunities and is less competitive when launching a new technology.

A team of business veterans with an insider knowledge of the German market.

Medica has been used as a major event to make preliminary contacts with partners.

Direct model for German distribution partners for other countries, where a local partner is better positioned to offer support in a local language.

'Countries that are smaller are perceived as easier
to manage from a start-up perspective.
It means they can manage demand in the
short term and not be overwhelmed.
It will be easier to fulfill orders.'

Eastern Europe, as an emerging market in the lab sector, has been chosen, as it is a less competitive road and a good way to meet demand gradually as production ramps up.

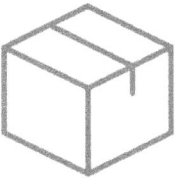

Product

'The main innovation came from the two founders,
whose main previous experience came from aerospace
and Formula 1 racing. And these two backgrounds,
combined with a concern for public health, triggered
the development of a major innovation.'

Fluxergy is offering a breakthrough technology in the laboratory sector. This is a multiplatform point-of-care diagnostic technology. The main innovation came from the two founders, whose main previous experience came from aerospace and Formula 1 racing. And these two backgrounds, combined with a concern for public health, triggered the development of a major innovation. The Fluxergy testing platform is a highly integrated detection system which gives the capability to perform many different types of tests at the point of care. It can detect genes, molecules, chemicals and cells, with the same analyzer. The component changing is the cartridge. Each cartridge contains a different type of test, from infectious diseases such as COVID, to sexually transmitted diseases and other types of infections. It can also be used to monitor and manage chronic disease.

For the entry into the European market, the company was focusing on two specific offers at the time of the interview:

- COVID-19 PCR tests

- equine tests for horses.

Portability and affordability were the key drivers that were brought to the product by the experience in the electronics business by the main investor John Tu. In addition, long-standing business collaborations in the IT industry since the 90s with Bernd Schnell, based in Germany, brought international thinking from the initial conception of the product.

This means there has not been any need to customize the technology for the European market. What was critical to be able to start the commercialization of the technology in Europe was compliance, specifically obtaining CE-IVD (done in March 2021) for the COVID-19 test.

Some minor aspects were also adjusted quite early around adding some extra care to the packaging of the products to make sure the package shipped from California arrived in excellent condition in Europe.

In other words, the product was not fully ready for commercialization at the time of the interview, as you may have noticed. Fluxergy was still waiting for the compliance of their product. The timing is always critical when it comes to commercialization in the European market. For Fluxergy, given they were well resourced and could afford to adjust their timing to the compliance date, I assume this was not so much of an issue.

However, for most SMEs, this is critical. My long history working with SMEs is that compliance is not always addressed early enough. And sometimes, SMEs play catch up, as they have triggered interest of customers, and only then do they worry about which standards they have to comply with. The topic of compliance is often overlooked by SMEs.

Most SMEs in the medical sector are usually very well informed and equipped to handle the topic of compliance. Other industries are not always up to speed, in my experience. The tricky part is to synchronize the timeframe of compliance with the commercialization effort. You cannot sell a product to Europe if it's not compliant. This is true for most products and should be addressed early. The issue is that certification timelines are often beyond the control of the manufacturer or software developer. So planning for a product launch date in the European market may be tricky. To justify the cost of compliance and to recover its costs, it's critical to prepare a successful commercialization. Sometimes you can use the pre-commercialization stages to evaluate market response, to gather feedback and refine your strategy. It will help your business accelerate commercialization when compliance is received. In the next pillar, Customer, you will learn how Dr Tinazli used this pre-commercialization period.

Another interesting point that Dr Tinazli highlighted with Fluxergy, and that I have observed in many breakthrough innovations, is the fact that innovation came from another industry. The founders were not specialized in the lab sector. They brought their own perspective from other industries (aerospace, racing) to the diagnostic industry. That's how a new perspective is brought to an industry. This is also what happened in Australia when the biomedical engineers, ex-Resmed, started to look at respiratory protection in the industry. That's often how an innovation emerges.

Customer

The main target customers for Europe are laboratory services in two different applications: equine and human. Before the pandemic, they were very close to launch with the equine product. On the human side, there was a focus on COVID-19 tests.

In the healthcare market, hospitals are traditionally fairly conservative. This was not a major change in comparison with the US market. The approach to the market was first to stick to the core specifications, and transparency in communication.

As the CE-IVD was obtained shortly after the interview, the actual commercialization process of the technology had not started at the time of the interview.

'In terms of pricing, being in early stages, the strategy was to be probing the market for the right price point.'

'That simply means being initially on temporary pricing for a pilot project. Then, depending on customer traction, readjusting the strategy. It enabled us to see what the market was willing to pay for a certain product. On the other hand, it gave time to sharpen Fluxergy's pencils and get a better cost structure over time.'

> Probing the market before commercialization by test pricing with partners is a great idea. There are several European regulations that state that even free products and during trials the products need to comply with the regulation. So what's permitted pre-compliance is a good thing to check.

> In my view, when having two distinct product lines that target two different end-users, best practice is to just focus on one, do it well and then start the second market.

Country

> *'Countries which are smaller are sometimes easier*
> *to manage because, as a start up, you may be*
> *overwhelmed with too much demand so that means*
> *it's really about finding a country which is not so big*
> *that it may be difficult to meet the scale or meet the*
> *demand at the very beginning.'*

In a start-up environment, the choice of countries is strategic, as manufacturing capacity is progressively scaling up. Fluxergy has an interest in countries which are establishing new lab infrastructures, and are high growth in terms of infrastructure generally. **Countries that are smaller**

are perceived as easier to manage from a start-up perspective, in order to manage demand in the short term and not be overwhelmed. It will be easier to fulfill orders.

In that context, Eastern European countries are more open, 'new and fresh'. They ended communism only 30 years ago. There are good opportunities to build new and better infrastructure. Greece also has had some traction.

More established Western European countries have an old and established laboratory infrastructure that is saturated. But due to the strong connection of the investor, advisor and management teams, who are German nationals, it has naturally brought Germany as a first priority for the European market.

The objective is to scale Europe-wide in the medium term.

The Eastern European markets are often overlooked, because most of them are a bit smaller than the larger Western economies. This is true when you look at the total addressable market – larger markets are more attractive. It's smart for Fluxergy to choose to service smaller markets first in order to pace demand with production capacity as it is ramping up.

But I'd like to draw your attention to another variable, which is the appetite of a market. This is an important factor to address when selecting the right country for your solution. This is why combining desktop research with clever indicators (in Dr Tinazli's case, the number of new labs built) and with a practical field test to measure the level of response of a market is a useful exercise. This is how sometimes you can be surprised to obtain better results from unexpected markets!

Channels

This is still work in progress. For the channel partners the selection criteria have been established as follows. The distribution partners need first to see the potential beyond COVID-19. **It is important for Fluxergy to develop partnerships with a longer term view.** They need to have either a human health specialty and/or an animal health specialty.

At the time, Dr Tinazli's approach was that in countries where speaking the local language is important, a distributor will be required. Whereas in Germany, end-users, such as private hospitals and lab chains, can be approached directly. Dr Tinazli highlights that the distribution strategy is still being developed.

However, the key areas that are highlighted by Dr Tinazli are:

- A distributor should not just be about price.

- Distributors must understand the need for market development. They can develop their own creative ways to expand market penetrations into a broader use of PCR testing in more market segments.

- They show signs of commitment; for example, a partner in the Czech market developed an approach to market PCR tests to physician offices and explained in Czech how to conduct point-of-care testing.

The decision to go direct or not is strategic for a small business. Going direct means that sufficient local technical and sales resources need to be allocated for a successful entry. Things like choosing to set up a local entity and assessing if selling from your country of origin is well accepted by your European customers are some of the things to think about. From the perspective of Dr Tinazli, with the senior team being very experienced in the German market, this country is intended to be direct.

Then distributors in other European countries will be appointed to provide better support in the local languages. I will add that in some cases, it may make sense to still have distributors even if you have a local team with local expertise. In our experience with our customers, that has been a very common and successful model. In terms of defining distributor profiles, you may want to add selection criteria such as: the technical skills they need to possess, the customers they should have contracts with, the level of after-sales service they should be able to offer, and the range of complementary products they should offer in their range. These are a good start. In addition, as Dr Tinazli outlines, a very important criteria is their level of engagement and motivation – this can only be found out after a few months of working together. This is why an ability to exit if the partner does not perform is useful.

Team

'Moving from a corporate world to a start-up world was a fun challenge. It was an interesting learning curve to see that you may not always get an answer with the email domain name of a start-up!'

The founders and advisors at Fluxergy are **high caliber and experienced, with experts brought in with a global perspective from day one**. Key persons at Fluxergy have global connections.

The main investor, John Tu, born in Taiwan, studied in Darmstadt Germany, and speaks German. Bernd Schnell, advisor, based in Frankfurt, is highly experienced in information technology distribution, particularly in electronics. Bernd has been a long-standing advisor to John Tu.

Four people based in the US are dedicated to sales and marketing globally. For Europe, Dr Ali Tinazli is the Chief Commercial Officer. Bernd Schnell is a General Manager Europe and an advisor to the business. Dr Seidler is an advisor to the business based in Germany, particularly for the animal health market segment.

The profile of the team is an interesting one. In my experience, striking a balance between a team from the corporate world bringing structure to a business and the experience of operators that have worked in a smaller organizations, like start-ups or SMEs, is useful to start things from scratch. The team needs to know how to build sales with little means and be resourceful.

Marketing

Dr Tinazli has not been able to conduct intensive marketing because Fluxergy was still waiting for the CE-IVD approval at the time of the interview. So marketing of the product had not started yet.

As a preparation exercise, Dr Tinazli identified **Medica as a main avenue for future marketing**. He attended the virtual Medica conference in 2020. He spent quite a lot of time screening a list of companies.

On the back of his research, he set up 40 meetings. The goal was to start building the foundation for the European business, and to establish and maintain good communication with the connections made to create good trustworthiness.

According to Dr Tinazli, this type of show gives you a very good impression of what the market wants and needs. It also gives the opportunity to learn how to improve your criteria for selecting the right candidates for partnerships.

One of the interesting comments that was made by Dr Tinazli was to make sure that potential partners really have a history in the business of healthcare. He commented that during the pandemic a lot of companies were opportunistic about it, but did not really have the necessary credentials in healthcare to be serious partners.

He sees as part of the marketing strategy giving keynotes at events and increasing the Fluxergy web presence as two key elements.

It's been a constant over the 17 years that I have worked with exporters in the European market that international trade shows of the caliber of Medica have been instrumental in the success of exporters. They enable companies to build strategic partnerships, and are a very convenient way to meet and build relationships with your European distributors. This is where innovative distributors go when they are looking for a new product to add to their range. This is why these shows are very important. Despite the emergence of virtual conferences in recent years, I can confirm that virtual shows are not as efficient as in-person events in terms of lead generation and to build relationships. In-person also works best for product launches.

Dashboard

The business is fully funded by a unique investor, John Tu. It uses customer relationship management software to track progress and performance.

> This is an unusual and a very good place to be – a start-up fully funded from day one.

Futramed: a key opinion leader approach prior to fully establishing a distribution model focused on just one market: France

> They realized that until they can trigger some interest from end-users and some track record is built, none of the distributors will open the door. Futramed has focused on first building strong relationships with key opinion leaders before even starting to build their distribution network.

Is It Time to Start Exporting to Europe?

Focus on building relationships with French key opinion leaders.	Priority on achieving CE prototype built for field testing.	Focus on France, as the technology originated with a French scientist.
Initially one of the co-owners moved to Europe to create the relationships.	Where they think they are lagging at the moment.	Priority is on end-users prior to establishing channels.

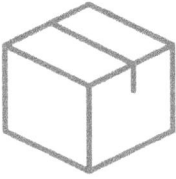

Product

As the founder, Doug Harding, is an engineer, **Futramed has put a lot of effort into the conception of the device**. In addition, Doug has surrounded himself with engineering and regulatory professionals. The objective was to get the features of the device perfect, with possible back-ups, even before they thought about launching the product.

Their utmost priority was to give to doctors a device that was CE marked. They did some early pre-commercialization field testing with a beta version of the product. They took the devices to pain clinics. This initial phase had about 12 prototypes field tested, which enabled them to improve the product.

So they felt that the final product they applied for the CE mark with was very strong. One of the main milestones was receiving the CE mark in 2020. They have the confidence the product is strong and well adapted for the European market for this reason.

They have a very strong value proposition, which they validated with field tests.

'We had some academic scientific indications of the efficacy and the safety of our product, and what that enabled us to do is to engage open-minded physicians who were looking for solutions to problems that they weren't able to overcome in another way.

'One of the doctors in a pain clinic commented that there were some patients who were taking opioids for pain, for example. They would be encountering a ceiling effect. By the time they would take x amount of opioid they would no longer receive any more pain relief. And it would start to compromise some of their normal body functions.

'What this device has the potential to do is at least maintain the pain relief that they were receiving from the opioids while allowing them to drop the dose. Some say by 10%, others say by 50%, depending on the opioid. Doctors are really looking for solutions in that field.'

The bigger the focus on end-user feedback, the stronger the value proposition about the product is. In my experience, European prospects will start to trust you when you can share with them the experience of your customers with your products. To gain trust with them you need to outline the issues that they are facing; it needs to resonate with them. Not only should you understand in depth the issues faced by your industries, but you should also be open to listen and understand what specific issues your European prospects have to manage and solve for. This is the only way to be able to adjust and communicate the right value proposition that is going to resonate with the European market. What's very unusual with Futramed is their choice to focus on France first before their domestic market. It would be more usual for an exporter to have an established domestic market before venturing into Europe. You can then use your deep understanding of your domestic customers' issues. Building your value proposition in the first instance from your domestic market and demonstrating how your solution has solved issues for your customers will certainly be a strong starting point for your European market. European potential customers will value your understanding of their industry, but then quickly acknowledge that their country certainly has specific issues. That is how you open the conversation about their issues and try to find common ground. This way you can detect how your solution will assist them.

Customers

'I placed a lot of emphasis on cultivating personal relationships with the KOLs, not only at the business level but I also got to know them personally.'

As Matt was living in Spain in 2012, he started to build his relationship with a neuroscientist, the 'right hand man' of the French physicist Aimé Limoge. The relationship grew as he was helping with the development of the device, as he had done the most current experiments on rats and humans.

Once they had a working prototype, Matt's mission was to identify the first early adopter of the technology. Dr Stinus was then able to put Matt in touch with an addiction association, and pointed him towards a specific conference in Vienna. His focus was to build relationships with psychiatrists and professionals working with addiction issues.

Prior to a conference, Matt would directly reach out through emails to some of the researchers. He made sure to meet them face to face at these conferences. They came from all different parts of France. And some of them showed a real interest in what Futramed was doing. That is how they built a solid network in France. Matt placed a lot of emphasis on cultivating these personal relationships, not only at the business level but he also got to know them personally.

A strong key opinion leader strategy is certainly a great way to stay tuned with the pulse of your market. It's where it all starts. And that builds a much stronger case for distributors to jump in. This is certainly something we have not always seen when we meet with companies that have ventured into Europe, notably in the medical sector. A lot of the time, a full mandate is given to the distributors to keep contact with end-users. This is a wrong approach in so many ways. First, your business only learns through the lens of the distributors, and it may be biased. Secondly, in the medical sector, for so many compliance reasons direct access to end-users is important. Thirdly, direct access to end-users builds your independence from distribution. If a distributor does not perform, end-users still have access to you, the manufacturer, if need be. It is a safer way to enter the European market.

Country

'We selected France as our first market as there is already a track record for the use of that technology in France. There's a good amount of peer-reviewed literature on that technology from as early as the late '60s. That gives us a lot of confidence.'

They have initially targeted Europe, because at the time in 2015–16, a lot of American medical device companies would start launching their products in the European market even before they would consider the American market. At the time, the American FDA approval process for their specific type of devices was much more arduous than the European market. Now things have changed, and the approval process has now become slightly harder in Europe. So now it is rather the opposite. Since they had already started down that path, they decided to persist and continue to focus on the European approval – the CE mark.

They initially opened a branch in Europe, based in the Basque country. As soon as the commercialization is in full swing, they are ready to use this entity.

Given the strong relationships that had been developed in France, Doug and Matt would like to pursue this goal. In addition, one of the reasons they are starting in France is because there's still a handful of highly esteemed professionals that are familiar with the technology due to the breakthrough of the French physicist Aimé Limoge.

Another reason they selected France as their first market is that there is already a track record for the use of that technology in France. There's a good amount of peer-reviewed literature on that technology from as early as the late '60s. That gives them a lot of confidence.

On a lighter note, Doug and Matt have a 'romantic' view that this technology that was invented in France should first be commercialized and successful in France.

The two key reasons for Futramed to focus on France are compelling. First, the level of awareness in the French market of their technology. And then at the initial stages, the easier pathway to getting CE rather than FDA approval.

Channels

As they are now in the middle of product trials, they believe that once this is done, end-users will help identify the right distributors. They have conducted some initial distributor research, notably through AmCham and some consultants, as well as by talking with businesses like Exportia. And **they realize that until they can trigger some interest from end-users and a track record is built, none of the distributors will open the door.** They think that having sold a few units will give them more leverage for engaging distributors.

> Channel strategy will come in time, once the interest of French key opinion leaders is fully secured. Then the purchasing process with French hospitals will guide the decision on the choice of a distributor. The distribution piece, in my view, should not be left too late, to make sure there is no impediment to sales.

Team

In terms of resourcing a team, since Matt has developed strong ties with doctors, he is thinking of continuing to nurture and look after these relationships. And the Futramed marketing team has more experience in building the distribution model.

Having one of the two business owners based in the market has been ideal. But a local team could supplement some of the commercial discussions with a distributor, for example. In many sectors where my business Exportia is playing, we find that founders of a business have an appetite to talk technology and to demonstrate the value of their products, whether they are engineers, an inventor or a medical professional. Sometimes, they find it harder to pursue pure commercial discussions to close deals. It is not so much of an issue at the preliminary stages of the entry to the European market, but down the track this is critical for commercial success. It's particularly true for early-stage businesses.

Marketing

This is probably where Futramed has done the least. They have been introduced to key medical and academic associations and attended conferences. This was their main marketing avenue and has proven to be very successful in connecting them to the right subject matter experts in the French market. **Marketing is where they feel they are lagging.**

This is where I am not that fussed. In our experience a huge amount of marketing is not always needed at the start. Having a sharp brand image – with the minimum market collateral that outlines your company history, your product features and your value proposition in a short brochure – is enough to start. This brochure can then be formalized in a short slide deck that can be displayed on a screen at a trade show.

For Futramed, it was a smart move to focus on local, highly specialized conferences where the French key opinion leaders gather and look out for information about their specialty. Smaller, highly specialized conferences are a great place to build relationships with the right key opinion leaders, and sometimes they are cheaper than large shows.

Dashboard

Fundraising is now being conducted. Business planning will really depend on the first product trials that were starting in the French market as the interview happened. The feedback from the trials is critical to the next business planning phase, and will influence the amount needed from the capital raising.

Joe L.: a software business that was able to accelerate its success in Europe via a better localization of the product and having local teams

Started in the UK for language reasons. But France was more open minded about buying from an American-based business. And in the end the largest single-European market for their technology is really Germany.	The channel partners model is the best way to plug in larger ecosystems (SAP, Salesforce, etc.). Their choice was to set up a network for implementation partners.
A multi-currency, multi-lingual version of their SaaS product made a big difference in their success.	They attend specialized industry events. Their marketing materials are done in English, then they will do them at least in French and German too. They found buying databases much harder in Europe than in the US.
Very large corporates are the target for this solution. Initially, large corporates in the US opened some doors in Europe.	They really started to have some success when they had a French person for the French market and a German person for Germany.

How each company approached the European market

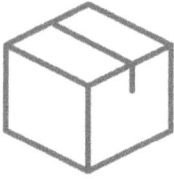

Product

> *'Your software may be as interesting and 'as simple as you think', but having different currencies and different languages all within one version is key.'*

A localized solution was the key to European success. The business that Joe works for has developed a cutting-edge software technology. Joe says that part of the attractiveness of this solution for international customers is that it talks the 'international language of numbers.'

One key success factor for the business in international markets, and notably Europe, was to move 10 or 11 years ago to a software as a service (SAAS) platform. They OEM'ed (integrated the capabilities) of world-renowned platforms to be able to internationalize their solution. Prior to that, the business was used to delivering an on-premise solution.

They knew that typically when it comes to software, the US will be the first country to adopt.

'Your software may be as interesting and 'as simple as you think', but having different currencies and different languages all within one version is key. It was really difficult for us, and we struggled. What made us make the investment was we kind of forced English upon some non-English-speaking countries and it just didn't work.

'Part of the learning in that process was to define the minimum set of languages: Italian, French, German and Spanish. Internationalization was always a secondary thought, and then it basically moved. Now, the minute we are going to offer a new feature, right away we would ask: can we do that in French, in German? Where are we limited? Can we do that in euros?'

In the software industry, the user interface is the first contact for your potential customer with the product. The easier the access for them, the faster you will be able to convince a potential buyer, and then once the purchase is approved, the easier the adoption of your product will be. As Joe explained, the question is: which product to start with? How many languages?

Before we get into the question about the choice of languages, I would like to underline the importance for software developers to anticipate the fact that their software will have to be translated into multiple languages. They have to take into account that each field will require different types of characters: it's obvious for many people that for Japanese and Chinese the characters will be different, but the same applies for European languages. The three main families of languages – Romance, Germanic and Slavic – have slightly different characters and accents that need to be antici-pated. The software fields need to take into account more characters than just for English words. The process of trans-lation must be made easy. The fewer words in your interface the better, and the more cost effective it will be to translate.

Translation should really not be an impediment – ideally you want to have a list of English terms exported into a table for a translator that can then be easily imported back by a software developer. The correspondence between English and the other language can then be easily recognized and allow a fast translation process. Translation should be an easy piece if it is well planned by the developers. That's the easy part in my view.

A cost-effective way to proceed is to select a country of focus, where you have validated that there is potential for your product. Once you have tested the interest, it's time to deliver the interface for that country. Then once you move to the next country, you repeat the process. In Joe's business, early on they identified their main markets were France, Germany, Italy and Spain, and they just went ahead and translated into the multiple languages. This is also a good way to proceed, if you can afford it.

In some industry sectors, and if your software has to comply with a European regulatory norm, it will be compulsory to have a user interface in the local language of the country you are selling to, so be aware that it may not even be an option not to translate.

Customers

The business mainly targets large corporates. **Initially, the business was able to lean on having success with US companies and then finding the large corporates' business units in Europe.** Having them as referrals for European prospects was helpful. But what really helped the business was having successful implementations in Europe. Being able to prove that the business was starting to show a commitment to the market helped immensely. Joe realized as well that while Americans are aware that Texas behaves differently to California, it's not *that* different. The differences between how European customers from different countries behave is much more significant than he anticipated. All Europeans know that Germany doesn't behave like France, for example.

It is important to realize these cultural differences early. In my business, we come across a lot of US businesses that set up in one country, set up a team there and expect that they will be able to cover multiple countries. But we Europeans know that a talented German salesperson who does not speak French will achieve very little success. Or it will take significantly more time. It's not only about being fluent in your customers' language, it's also about knowing how business is done there and what the dynamic is in that market.

When European companies realize it's good technology, they see the value of your product and you show that you are trending towards growing in Europe and you're eventually going to make that investment, it makes a big difference, rather than just putting together a team of Americans to come and implement anywhere within Europe.

European customers like to see that the non-European supplier they are buying from is making a long-term commitment to their market. It's particularly important when selling to large corporates. Buyers want to have reassurance that the solution they are buying and implementing has some perennity. Showing long-term local investment demonstrates dedication and serious engagement in Europe.

Joe did not see that being a US company was an impediment to the business. The leadership in the business is very result focused.

'Once we started to have commercial success we proved that we could do it and we are all in. There were some challenges of being part of an up-and-coming software company selling to very large, well-known names. It also made it pretty easy for us to bring people in.

'We historically have not hired junior people; we hire very seasoned professionals, very experienced salespersons, software salespersons in B2B who understand science.'

Country

'The business initially went to the UK, because it was the same language and it made it easy to recruit. It became pretty obvious that England specifically (not all of the UK, but specifically just England) had all the right types of companies, as did France.

'The French in general were more open to dealing with American-based companies, and so they were more open minded and the business had some success there.

'But one big total addressable market that we struggled with was Germany. At one point, we had a French seller selling into Germany and it just wasn't working effectively.

'We tried to sell into other European countries, but we're a bit expensive and so probably companies less than €250 million in revenue wouldn't buy but anybody above that would and then a decent percentage of our customers are above a billion euro. So pretty quickly that rules out a lot of countries and, if you start looking at the concentration of where those companies are, it's definitely in France, Germany and England.

'The main European market for the business is now Germany.'

It's a typical move to enter the UK market first because of the English language. I personally love the UK and the Brits, but in business terms, American, NZ, Australian and South African businesses tend to go to the UK first because of the language proximity. It is a mistake not to conduct a full assessment and to test a shortlist of carefully selected countries before entering the European market. It saves a huge amount of time and money to focus first and foremost on the country that has the best potential and appetite for your product and solution. That should be the only criteria to decide which market to focus on first. In this instance, France has been faster to take off.

'Germany was the country that eluded us for years. I think there were times that we did hire German sellers. Now that we're starting to have success, I think it really is about having someone native to German culture. It makes German customers feel like they're going to be taken care of as a company. And running alliances was effective. I've spent a lot of time trying to get our consulting partners and our software partners that are in Germany to be involved in the sales cycle. In addition to that, Germany has more software companies (more than France, for example), starting with SAP and other software companies that have spun off SAP.

'When it comes to software, I think the Germans are very particular and, if possible, would rather buy software from a German-based software company. So not having anybody even based in Germany just made it that much more difficult. Local European competition was stronger in Germany. But some of the traditional American competitors of that business went straight to Germany and set up offices there, so that made it even more difficult.'

The German market is in general terms the largest in the European market, because of its large population and also because of its very solid and dense industry. However, it often looks attractive on paper, but is also very competitive. It is a hard nut to crack. It's interesting to note that investing in native German sellers really helped. And as the success builds up it helps to attract better talent. Once a small local team is in place, it builds the capability to leverage a local network of influencers in the market. In this case, Joe is mentioning their ability to create a network of local alliances around the SAP network. Assessing the appetite of a market and testing it will enable you to reveal the competitors' dynamic: how strong are they, how crowded is the market, are customers desperate for a new player to enter this market? These are important factors for a business to decide: where should I go first? The way we make these decisions in my business is that we typically select two top markets. We test both to determine which one is more likely to generate revenue the fastest. We start with the market with the biggest appetite – the market that is ready to buy now – to generate revenue. Once we have done that we move to the second market, and so on. Your best market – in Joe's example, Germany – may be the largest, but at the same time it's the one that will take a lot of time to build. Indeed, in his case, Germany is where his largest American and European competitors are very active, making it more challenging for his business to enter.

The smaller your business is, the faster you want to generate revenue, and it's therefore critical to keep both market size and market appetite in mind, before you choose your market of focus.

Sales channels

'One of Joe's learnings to successfully drive revenue from these large multinational channel partners is to really work with the people who are actively doing the sales.'

In their European strategy and more broadly in their international strategy, they have set people in different countries to target large corporate accounts. In addition to that, Joe mentions that they have established channel partners. However, these partners don't actually resell, they are **implementation partners**. They are **management consulting partners**.

So for Joe it is a matter of connecting the business's salespersons with the SAP salesperson, or with the Salesforce salesperson, or the Deloitte one, and so on. This is the way these big companies think. For example, SAP has a German country manager, and everyone underneath this person is focused on Germany, so having a counterpart that focuses just on Germany is what really works. The same could be said for France or England, and even Italy.

The whole strategy of running alliances is to **plug into bigger eco-systems**. So Joe spends a lot of time becoming a strategic partner with SAP, Salesforce and Oracle, just because that's where the majority of his customers are. If you look at the size of customers Joe's business would target, they would typically make investments as follows: in the back office they'll either be Oracle or SAP, and in the front office Salesforce CRM, and then some of the other products with a sprinkling of other vendors.

> Plugging into larger ecosystems is a way to accelerate sales and access large sales teams.

Working with these large partners (such as Salesforce or SAP) is not easy. To be successful in those situations, you have to find your experts per region.

One of Joe's learnings to successfully drive revenue from these large multinational partners is to really work with the people who are actively doing the sales.

For example, Salesforce is broken into 'clouds'. So if it's the revenue cloud, find out who the revenue cloud B2B expert is in Europe. Those people will work across countries, so what Joe found to be the most advantageous is dealing with people that are responsible for sales. Having people who are in partner roles may not always help from a sales perspective, what they'll help with is doing introductions, scheduling meetings, maybe making sure that you're part of certain marketing collateral. But, the only way you'll impact sales is if you're dealing with people that are responsible for sales.

So even if it's not easy, essentially Joe tries a local approach too. That's when a local UK strategy, a French strategy and a German strategy comes into play. That is what guides success for the business;

for example, Joe won't spend any time trying to develop a relation-ship with Oracle in Germany, as he knows that SAP wins all the time, however partnering with Salesforce in Germany is absolutely the right focus.

> I think this is gold for any business. Whether you are a manu-facturer working with a distributor or a software developer and vendor working with channel partners, the key is to connect and work with your partners' local sales teams. They are your extended sales engine – if they develop a vested interest in selling your product, if you train them well enough to become comfortable with selling your solution, you are going to accelerate sales and achieve quicker success.

At the time of the interview, Joe had been doing this for about four years. And some of his learning is quite interesting. Initially, he went to the big consulting partners – to people that he thought knew their business, but Joe's business had a lack of market awareness. It was their biggest problem. **The biggest competitor to his business was 'doing nothing'.**

When companies need an enterprise resource planning system, it's different – the need is already identified and they need to pick a supplier. When it comes to the solution provided by Joe's business, you could continue to try to do it in spreadsheets. You might be doing it ineffectively. You might be losing margin. But you can still do it. As Joe started realizing that, he thought that really the way to grow was through software partners. So he started with Salesforce and found the right area to dive in and develop relationships from there.

Once he felt that was up and running, he went to SAP and Oracle and tried managing both. Then he focused on SAP.

The channel partner model in the software industry is quite mature. Typically, large software vendors – such as SAP, Salesforce, IBM, Oracle and Microsoft – have a very mature structure for their partner ecosystem. For software that has the capability to plug in a major independent software vendor solution, or to be complementary, it's a great way to access larger ecosystems.

Joe needed to grow the SAP partnership. One of Joe's business's traditional competitors in Germany was a very high level partner with SAP. Whenever you get to this level of partnership, SAP won't partner with any of the partner's competitors. So for years, the SAP world was closed to Joe's business.

But SAP disbanded that relationship in 2016. At that point, Joe made SAP his number one ecosystem to grow. He knew that with this partner out, there was opportunity. And everyone was going to try to get in there. Joe did some research. That's how he came across a specialist and long-established SAP ecosystem expert (Ralf Meyer) and decided to hire him to aim to get somewhere in 12 months, instead of what would normally take him 36 months. And he thinks he wouldn't have been as effective without Ralf. He helped Joe grow the strategy: where to focus, learning more about the SAP culture, what works, what doesn't work and leveraging Ralf's overall experience as well.

Team

> *'About hiring in Europe, we went as far as we could with English speakers until we thought it was hurting us in terms of business not to have French and German speaking skills.'*

Joe's business started making a significant investment in hiring locally about 11 years ago – they went from just one salesperson to multiple salespeople, implementation people, customer success people. Which is where they're at now.

They started to hire in the following way. They knew they needed a manager to run the business, like a general manager. So they took somebody who was an experienced leader in the US, who knew the product well, had sold it and had learned to implement it. And they made that person the general manager.

And they started hiring people from there. This general manager was able to help new people get trained up by either doing it themselves or by being able to contact their counterpart within the North American office. And from there, every six months they had some of the US-based leaders go out to Europe to do product updates, use implementation learnings from other customers, and more. They started growing that way.

They went as far as they could with English speakers until they thought it was hurting them not to have French and German speaking skills.

The US being an English-speaking country, it just made sense for them to headquarter initially in London. Knowing that the people they sell to are more senior within their organization, it's common for Joe's business to sell into the C-suite or at the Director level. They knew that while it might not have been a preference, in France, Germany and Belgium the executives would likely speak English. And that's how they started.

As they started supporting the sales cycle, it became pretty obvious that they needed to hire someone with French skills, then they needed to hire someone with German skills.

According to Joe, they really went as far as they could until they thought that it was hurting them.

While hiring, being part of an up-and-coming software company already selling to very large, well-known names made it easier for them to bring people in. What also helped was the fact that they are in a space that's been growing, so they didn't have any problems hiring people.

Historically they have never hired junior people, they have hired very seasoned professionals. If it's a salesperson, they would be a very experienced software salesperson in B2B that understands science. They have always invested in senior proven people in Europe at least to start off.

As mentioned by Joe, initially they sent US managers to travel back and forth to set up the European business. It was a safe choice from the technical side. In addition, having a trusted person in a senior role is also a good way to start a business. The choice of the UK as the entry country to hire from initially was driven by language and by the knowledge that the UK market is home to many corporates, the size of which is needed by Joe's business. Ultimately, as he recognized, you can only go so far without the language skills in France and Germany. In our experience, non-European businesses that work with our European team only realize the extent of what they have missed when they have an 'insider' in their team. That is when they actually realize how much they are missing out on in terms of understanding of the market. A deep 'native' understanding of a market and its culture removes significant barriers, it helps to detect buying signals faster, and it also allows more honest conversations. And problems can often be solved more easily in one's native language. It means that for non-European businesses, having someone on your team take you through this local navigation always accelerates success. This is why Joe mentions that it is really only when they started to have local Europeans that things shifted and they could reach new heights.

The other dynamic that is quite important and that was alluded to by Joe was that Germany eluded them for years. And when he looks back, he knows why. He had hired a French senior salesperson, and he had a team of American managers to enter the German market.

As a strategy to set up in Europe, they decided to hire quite senior people from the start. They would hire one seasoned salesperson and one seasoned service person, and trust them to sell around Europe.

Joe mentioned that they have some people in their business who came from a company similar to them, but more on the B2C side, not the B2B. Six or seven years ago, they were acquired by IBM and the culture started changing. And Joe's business started hiring them over. So the business did a decent amount of hiring on the sales side through their network.

On the services side, they did start by using recruiters, then quickly they began using their network here as well.

Because Joe's business area is very specialized (AI pricing), typically pricing people know other pricing people. They can just call around and ask if they know anybody in this country where they are hiring. Joe mentioned that they also have hired from their customers. After the project, professionals working for their customers would come to them and say they want to work for their business. Some other times a prospect might come along and they might not buy the solution, but the pricing professional would come back and say they would love to work for the business.

For sure using their network has been the most successful way to hire. It's always difficult to get a great candidate. If you hire from your network, your chances are better. When you are hiring leadership roles from your network, you know the type of leader they are. **The key takeaway from Joe is to splurge on good leadership.** Otherwise it's very hard to build an implementation practice or a sales practice.

I like the way Joe expresses it: 'splurging on good leadership'. I completely agree with the approach of first getting to know a market, achieving some level of success, and as you do that you keep your eyes and ears wide open to detect talent. In this case, Joe used the opportunity of sourcing candidates from another pricing business but in the B2C sector. This is a great way to hire. It adds good quality candidates to your pool of potential new employees. We use the same technique by observing how peers of our customers behave in a market.

There are sales teams out there today in a specific European country that are talking to your potential customers daily. They of course are your competitors, and I am not a big fan of hiring from competitors, because how loyal are these employees going to be? The other option is to detect sales teams that sell products that are non-competitive and complementary to yours. It's easy to liaise with them, exchange with them, build rapport and quietly assess them. When the business is ready to hire, you can signal the opportunity to this network. So I am a big advocate of using your network to hire, like Joe did.

Marketing

In terms of marketing, they went to specialized industry events. This way they obtained email addresses. Getting emails is definitely more difficult in Europe than it is in the US. Buying databases of contacts is much more difficult. The focus was more industry events and not necessarily mass mailings.

The business always invested in **inside sales**: having people on the phone trying to get meetings. The way they filled in the role of inside sales and having multilingual capabilities was through external companies. You don't necessarily need to be an expert to do inside sales, you just need to get that first meeting with the right level of person. So Joe's team would explain to them the type of persona they were looking for and the talking points.

According to Joe, at the lowest level, that was pretty effective. He thinks that to be effective selling on the phone, you need cultural fit. Otherwise it is going to be really difficult.

They have also prioritized sponsoring events that focus on their specific topic of pricing. For example, their industry society has an annual conference. One year, it's in the US, one year in Europe.

They also have marketing materials that are in French and German, as well as videos and demos. If they do them in English, they will do them at least in French and German as well.

Inside sales or lead-generation teams or appointment-setting teams have a lot of value in a technical sales cycle. When most engineers, scientists and medical professionals create a business, they often tend to think that you must be a specialist in their field like them to be able to sell their technology. That's not completely right. In sales, particularly when entering a new market, there are a lot of repetitive tasks and a lot of relationship building. It also comes down to articulating a short, sharp and clear message on the phone to a prospect. To do this type of activity is very time consuming and requires a lot of persistence, and there is not time to go into technical details. Therefore, these tasks can be done by a trained non-specialist, who can get the first meeting.

The other marketing strategy, sponsoring events, is a great way to generate exposure quite fast and be in front of the right people. Presenting at these events is a great way to attract the right type of customers too.

Another great medium chosen by Joe's business is videos. This is one of my favorites! A video is a great way to communicate, particularly to introduce a product or a new technology. It needs to be short, sharp and to the point. The great value of videos is that it's super easy to create a transcript in a different language. That is cost-effective marketing, and it can have a huge impact.

Dashboard

The business leverages their CRM system. This has allowed them over time to grow contacts and to manage the sales cycle. In their business, it's common to start a sales cycle and then three years later the customer comes back and says, 'we are ready to buy now'. So having that history in a CRM is essential.

On the sales side, they have a global leader, and also a European leader and a North American leader who report to the global leader. From a KPI perspective the dashboard is within the CRM.

Phoenix Medical Systems: being strategic about using the European market as a springboard for other markets

'I can't dispute the fact that yes, this is a big revenue earner. International businesses have better profit margins than what you sell in India.'

This example of Indian company Phoenix provides a very different approach to Europe. I find it extremely smart and interesting. Phoenix has a product range of baby warmers designed and manufactured in India, at a lower price point than its Western counterparts. This enables

Phoenix to be in a unique position to match the needs of a number of developing countries, with a great-quality product.

The Phoenix Medical Systems founder always had the ambition to take his business to global markets. As a dominant domestic player in the Indian market, they have very large volumes but find that the Indian market is very challenging in terms of margins and that export markets offer much better price levels.

When Vinod came along and joined the business, he thought one of the best ways to take the business to international standards and measure where it was in terms of international marketability was to exhibit at the largest global medical fair, Medica. At this point, they decided to transform their manufacturing process and take a big step towards reaching the quality standards required for the international markets with their European partner.

In addition, Europe was where the connection was made to companies that are responsible for sourcing equipment in large volumes for international institutions, such as UNICEF, as a lot of them have their headquarters in Europe.

An extraordinary effect of Phoenix going international has been for them to increase their international visibility. When they lifted their quality by working with the Swiss company, and then sold to UNICEF through a German company, they became visible to GE Healthcare as a solid player. It led to a major partnership with them, the global market leader, back in their home market in India.

The primary clients and end-users are the maternity departments of hospitals. There are two other direct customers for Phoenix, large international not for profits and international institutions funding and providing maternity equipment, as well as their preferred sourcing partners.	Focus on baby warmers with a distinctive and pleasing design (an oval shape) as well as a big shift towards better quality and continuous quality improvement in their manufacturing.	Europe is the place to connect with major international institutions that are then supplying Phoenix equipment around the world. Eastern Europe is where Phoenix is doing well.
Vinod is an astute export manager, who has built a lot of connections to take the export business of Phoenix where it is now.	Medica has been a decisive marketing event for them. They are now a regular exhibitor every year.	Distributors in Italy and in Eastern Europe. A large focus is placed on distributors' sales teams and their motivation plans to sell the Phoenix product.

How each company approached the European market

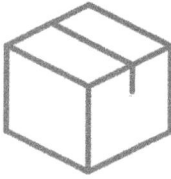

Product

> *'We did not replicate what the rest of the world
> was doing, we had our own in-house design guys.
> We stood apart from the rest of the world in terms
> of design, in terms of functionality and in terms
> of slightly higher features.'*

The founder of Phoenix wanted to provide innovation in a market where every single competitor offered the same incubators and the same warmers. He thought that there were not enough features designed more for the newborn. He wanted to integrate a whole lot of features into one item and to make it such that, besides a mother and father, you do not have to worry about anything else because the equipment itself will take care of the baby. So he brought about a lot of innovative features.

For this product, the competitors are majors such as Draeger, Siemens and GE Healthcare.

A very big Swiss company approached Phoenix and told them: 'What you've done is what we want, but manufacturing in Switzerland is going to be too costly. And you can do this for us at a fraction of a cost.' So Phoenix agreed to also manufacture the product under the Swiss company's brand name.

One of the reasons was that they wanted to learn more about how it should be done. At that point in time, the manufacturing practices were a little cruder than what they are today. Through this collaboration,

Phoenix as a business integrated a lot of learnings in terms of quality as well as in enabling faster delivery.

They involved the production team to make sure they would place special care on the orders from Switzerland, and to highlight how this was critical to the business's overall increase in quality.

> Phoenix has used the European market standards to lift their game and that has been critical for them in their international shift. It's interesting to see that, as the European market was not a short-term target region. They used this market to their advantage and to reach other larger markets such as several countries on the African continent.

Vinod mentions that what attracted international customers to their booth was the overall appearance of the product. They did not replicate what was going on in the market. They changed the design to make it close to the experience of the baby in the womb. They also thought of recreating the shape of the arm when holding a baby, again an oval shape, instead of having a traditional rectangular infant warmer like their competitors were designing. **This beautiful oval shape is very pleasing to the eye and does not have any sharp edges; everything is very curvy. That shape is a statement: we do not replicate what the rest of the world is doing.** The Phoenix design came from their own in-house design team.

Phoenix stood apart from the rest of the world in terms of design, functionality and having slightly higher features than what the rest of the world had to offer. Vinod thinks it is what made medical professionals stop by his stand at the major medical fair, Medica. Otherwise, they would have thought: 'Indian company, no I don't want to stop.' This in itself was a big success.

Unfortunately, Indian companies have to battle with a reputation for low-quality manufacturing. It is now changing due to major luxury brands such as Mercedes manufacturing in India. India has built over the last decades a reputation in technology sectors such as IT, which shone the light on India's capability to be at the forefront of innovation. This reputation has not transpired in other industry sectors, but I believe a significant shift should be seen in the coming decade, one of the reasons being the high level of education provided in India.

Therefore, it was important for Phoenix to make a point to have a product that met international standards. That's very commendable, and I am eager to see this business start to market their product around the world.

Customers

In 2004, their participation at Medica is how they attracted the attention of their first European customer from Switzerland. The OEM deal with the Swiss company lifted the quality of the manufacturing and then enabled Phoenix to get the attention of other players in the medical space. It still took six to seven years to attract the attention of other large European customers. They then had companies based in the Netherlands and in Germany starting to show interest and approaching them, as they began to see that Phoenix was a serious player, given their partnership with the Swiss company and also they had been active in the market for a number of years.

On this basis, they started to build a reputation as a company that can be molded into each customer's needs and as reliable. They attracted the attention of Dutch and German suppliers to UNICEF. That is how they started to supply to UNICEF.

> Persistence and regular presence at Medica – where every year visitors can observe the progress of the business, in their design, in the way they market their products – was vital to Phoenix. Our experience is that European buyers tour these shows and scan specific products they are interested in, and they monitor these products' evolutions yearly at trade shows. We often hear comments from buyers such as, 'Last year we did not stop, but we have watched your business grow every year and we now see that you have an interesting product. Tell me more about it.'

There was a random inquiry from a German company for a CPAP product for babies who are born premature. It gives a blend of air and oxygen through the nose of the baby to keep the lungs inflated. Originally this project company was sourcing CPAP devices from a German manufacturer; it was a wonderful product, but probably too advanced and the delivery times were very long. At that time the German manufacturer took almost six months to deliver one order. The German project management company was concerned UNICEF would end their contract and contacted Phoenix for a quote.

Vinod grabbed this opportunity and made it a priority. He told them he was able to **provide quicker delivery times**. And he said he suspected they were buying from this German company, that he knew what they made, and this is what Phoenix make, and he outlined his proposal in terms of quality and price. He also committed to delivery times and offered to get penalized if the delivery times were not met. That was exactly what the German project management company supplying to UNICEF needed. The delivery times were their main concern. So Vinod was able to make them comfortable to go to the next level with Phoenix.

This is something that is often overlooked. When a non-European business has to enter the European market and has to face very strong, well-established European and global competition, any crack is a way to get in. In that case the crack was long delivery times of the supplier. Vinod being on top of this request and shifting the priority of the business to make sure he could respond to this strategic enquiry paid off. This is not rocket science but it is critical.

At some stage, what was really interesting was that GE wanted to enter the Indian market. And, like any multinational, they wanted to find a local partner. India has a 1.3 billion population and the need for neonatal and maternal care devices is very big. And Phoenix is the biggest player in that market. Phoenix is extremely well settled in its home market. GE sensed that there was huge potential for these kinds of devices. So they approached Phoenix to partner.

They said: 'We are GE healthcare, we can do this, we can do that, if you're doing this, you can do six times your turnover or five times your current turnover.' But GE only would do it in their own brand name. This is where Phoenix refused, because it's a brand which they have built over the years. And just because an American multinational comes in and says so, did not mean that Phoenix had to accept.

Phoenix requested the products they manufactured be in their own brand name. Phoenix knew that GE did not understand how the Indian market works, how Indian sentiments work, how you have to mollycoddle customers in India. So, in summary, Vinod was quite proud to say that even the biggest companies in the world wanted to partner with Phoenix. And Phoenix snapped at GE and secured the partnership.[49]

> This is a recurring theme among our customers over the years: what they learn in Europe, or the changes prompted by exporting, also benefited the entire business.

He went on and explained how this second project with a European customer (German project management business) shaped their own expectations with their supply chain department and how it strengthened it. They had to stick to timelines. At the start, it was not great, but they learnt, and improved.

They also improved their entire supply chain when it came to the components bought from outside: they bolstered incoming goods inspections, they also bolstered packing and strengthened the entire supply chain process. Improved packing was a very important part as well to raise the quality of their delivery.

At some point, Phoenix decided to hire the Swiss manager they had as their first client, who was then retired. He looked at the factory and conducted a gap analysis. And needless to say, the list of what was wrong was more than the list of what was correct. And this is exactly why they called him in.

Following this gap analysis, they made significant investment in their manufacturing equipment, and it took the quality of the finished product to a whole new level.

49 www.ge.com/news/press-releases/ge-healthcare-signs-exclusive-agreements-phoenix-medical-systems-and-sle-uk.

How each company approached the European market

Country

Besides supplying to companies in Germany and the Netherlands because of the Phoenix product being a registered vendor for UNICEF, the rest of their European markets are mainly Eastern European countries. Phoenix is doing well in Romania, Bulgaria, and is starting in Albania. There are some marginal sales in Italy and France.

Channels

In comparison to India, Vinod found that European distributors do not negotiate as much. One of his key learnings was to have a successful distributor, and what really mattered was to **engage, motivate and incentivize** the sales teams. The management write the checks, but the sales team is selling your product.

At one point, his Italian distributor had lower sales than usual. He called the business owner. And he learnt that they still found the product fantastic, but they had just launched a new breast pump product line. So he realized they got a bit distracted. He told them he was very happy for them, but he could not have his sales suffer from such a drop. He asked to talk to the sales team about it, and to be put in touch with the person in charge of the Phoenix portfolio.

He asked if they were able to get any new prospects and asked if they faced any difficulties, and offered to provide some training. He also incentivized the person in charge of his portfolio. He coordinated the incentive plan with the boss of the business. So, he incentivized one person in that business, and he was able to double the sales in comparison to two years prior. Vinod thinks that you need to motivate somebody to do well.

> The approach of Vinod with his distributor's sales representative was spot on. Having direct access to the sales team is crucial to maintaining a successful distributor over time. Making sure they are trained and motivated and don't take their focus off your product is a constant effort that has to be made throughout the working relationship. It can take the shape of a sales motivation plan for a sales team, the creation of a plan together and regular check ins on the progress of the plan.

Team

In terms of team, at the time of the interview Vinod was the Senior Export Manager based out of South Africa. He has no team members based in Europe yet. He is using his distributor's sales teams to generate sales.

> The bulk of sales are conducted through a small number of key relationships with suppliers to the large international institutions. These strategic relationships are successfully managed by Vinod. The Eastern European and Italian distributors are working well but their volume does not justify an investment in the region for now. The resources allocated to a market should grow as the sales are picking up.

Marketing

Focusing on in-country specialist conferences, instead of large generic ones, creates traction with key opinion leaders and thus drives the interest of distributors.

In terms of marketing, Phoenix tend to launch new products at major trade shows, such as Medica and Arab Health. However, one of the main learnings from Vinod is instead of participating in general equipment shows such as Medica and Arab Health, where you have to be there, and you have to show that the company is large and growing – if he was to go to trade shows and conferences again (the interview was held during COVID), he would focus on the conferences that are only held in his specialty. Phoenix makes medical equipment for babies, so he would rather focus on neonatology conferences or pediatric conferences instead of registering for Medica.

> For the European market, Medica is the place to be to identify key buyers in the European medical sector. It is a distributor show. However, during the interview Vinod also mentioned that Phoenix must be seen at these trade shows by buyers every year. It's like an 'obligation to be seen', however Vinod and I agree that smaller, specialized conferences are also a cost-effective way. With my team, we have conducted a lot of smaller, low-key conferences where the target audiences were end-users. These specialized conferences can be powerful to switch a market on and drive and lock in distributor interest.

In terms of brand, **Vinod has leveraged the brand image of Chennai** as an advanced car manufacturing hub in India. It has driven the increased quality of the electronics and the labor. Chennai is where the Phoenix factories are located, and where Hyundai, Suzuki, BMW and Bosch are located. A lot of multinationals have established manufacturing in Chennai.

So Vinod is able to convey this brand image of quality thanks to the characteristics of Chennai.

Using packaging to reflect the quality of a premium product has also been a focus. Packaging creates the first impression. And it needs to convey quality. So Phoenix has focused on this too.

Frequent emails on new products is an efficient way to stay in touch. Vinod has a database of emails, which he sends out to every three weeks. People have a tendency to forget! So he likes to send them the latest product news and also updates on their latest technology partnerships, for example on a project with Stanford or about a project they are doing in New Zealand. These simple emailers create automatic business.

> These nurturing emails are a great way to stay in touch without being too salesy; prospects will be interested to know what the business is up to and it creates credibility about the business. The reality is that European specialists – like in the case of Vinod's specialists in neonate – will certainly be interested to know what Stanford is collaborating on with Phoenix. We often associate newsletters with spamming, but when you really curate your list and restrict it to your ideal target audience, and you deliver to them content that is really relevant, it's impactful . . . and cost effective!

Vigience: humility, intelligence and persistence drive success

Vigience has a unique story in Europe. The **humility** with which Markus has shared his experience taking his business to Europe shows his **intelligence** in business, as does his ability to shift and change, knowing when to take a step back, gather your learnings and thoughts and go again. His persistence has paid off. **Persistence** is a core quality that goes a long way in Europe.

The Vigience story in Europe occurred in two attempts.

The first time Vigience entered the European market, Markus created a local representative office in Switzerland because he thought that emotionally Europeans would never buy directly from a Japanese business. Being a Swiss native from the German-speaking part, he felt very comfortable focusing the business on the DACH region. There was a great cultural alignment. In Switzerland, he created a team composed of presales for demos, sales and implementation. This was a sizable European team, including some of his team relocating to Europe as well as some outsourced business development team members. He hired an excellent marketing agency to create marketing campaigns, and they attended trade shows.

As it turned out, in respect to the means and resources allocated, the business only generated a handful of clients. It was really hard to justify as a return on investment, even though early customers are important to a business.

In the second attempt, the approach was stripped down to one single priority: understanding the European customers' needs. Everything revolved around this and every part of the strategy was built around these very specific needs: marketing messages, channel partners and resources allocated.

My interpretation of the first attempt failure is that the market entry assumed that Europe would be the same for a corporation and for

Large manufacturers using SAP.	Out-of-the-box solution to connect SAP and Salesforce for manufacturers.
In their first attempt, they had established their own team as well as an outsourced team for business development and marketing. In the second attempt, the team is much leaner in Europe and Markus the CEO has been fully involved in the sales process.	In the first attempt, they had a large marketing campaign with an external marketing agency. They also exhibited at trade shows. In the second attempt, they focused on having the right marketing message built on their customers' needs.
DACH has been a major market from day one. However, Denmark has been an early adopter. Now the UK is also becoming a major market.	They decided to focus all their attention, energy and resources on building business with Salesforce only.
In terms of dashboards, it's a work in progress. They measure the number of deals closed.	

a start-up. Unbeknownst to Markus at the time, he used his excellent corporate career mindset and experience to plan his market entry. However, the means allocated to a market are often not enough to make it, even for large corporates. Many large US corporates have failed in Europe and have had to make several attempts.[50] The only difference between us start-ups/SMEs and large corporates is that we cannot afford to fail too many times!

Now I let you discover the full story of this successful strategy into the European market in two acts.

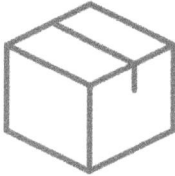

Product

> *'For the very first customers, I think you have to be very agile and be able to add features on the fly. I would sell this really great opportunity. And then the customer would require one feature that we don't have. You cannot say you don't have it, because then you lose that opportunity. If you don't have hundreds of opportunities to choose from, in a number of cases we'd throw the request to the team to add some feature required by the market. More or less overnight we delivered the feature, we really made that customer happy, and moved on.'*

---

50 Please refer here for the February article from the *Harvard Business Review* about US software businesses failing in Europe. hbr.org/2021/02/what-u-s-startups-get-wrong-about-expanding-into-europe.

When asked how the Japanese and the European markets differ, Markus mentions that European customers and Japanese customers like the same things in the product. **The difference is not so much what they're interested in, but how you get the attention of the customer, who you compete with and what you do in the given market.**

In Europe, Vigience solves the problem of deep connection between SAP and Salesforce. Given that in Europe they are SAP-heavy, they need very deep integrations. Vigience provides this out-of-the-box solution, so you don't need a big system integration project that can last a year or two. And in the case of large companies, this type of system integration project can cost millions of dollars.

System integrators don't have the resources anymore to understand SAP and Salesforce on that level.[51] Vigience provides integration that goes way beyond just collecting data between two systems. Vigience provides true business process integration. Once the Vigience team can show that to the customer, and that they can go live now and not in a year, and they can save money and headaches, they like to go with Vigience to get a fast start. Vigience customers may be specialists in building machines or some other product, but they're not specialists in doing highly complex software projects. This way, Vigience's customers also get a lot out of what Salesforce provides and they get a deep solution for salespeople, and for customer self-service and so on. So Markus thinks that's what they like.

In comparison to the Japanese version of the product, they added features for Europeans that were not required in Japan. In Europe, a lot of customers have an existing SAP middleware in place that they must use or want to use. So Vigience builds support for going through

51 System integrator definition from Gartner Group: An enterprise that specializes in implementing, planning, coordinating, scheduling, testing, improving and sometimes maintaining a computing operation.

that middleware and not directly integrating with SAP. It's specific to Europe because SAP is more rolled out in Europe than it is in Japan.

Europe also uses different features, for example for configurable products. They manage that in SAP. If you buy a car, you can pick the type of wheels, the colors and so on. These are configurations that live in SAP in Europe and not in Japan, so they had to add features like this.

> Vigience has completely adapted to the European market needs by adding Europe-specific features.

Generally speaking, in the case of the very first customers, Markus thinks **you have to be very agile and be able to add the features they require from you on the fly**. In the initial stages, you don't have hundreds of opportunities; if the customer requires one feature that you don't have, you just need to get the team to add it. It happened to him and his team while working on very large sales opportunities. If the market asks for it, more or less overnight they tried to make it happen and make the customer happy, to close the opportunity.

And then after three, four or five customers, Vigience started to see some requests repeating. Markus is a strong believer in **providing that level of flexibility to win deals at the beginning of your journey**.

This lesson he learnt and applied from experience. As he went for the first time to Europe in a partnership with a Japanese corporation, the decision-making process was very slow when he had to request a new feature. The customer said they would buy if they had this one feature. Then he had to go through the request process with his JV partner in Japan, get the budget, and it would take weeks to get the approval. By that time, he would have lost the customer.

During the second attempt entering the European market for Vigience, he was able to secure all the rights for the products. It meant that when a European customer asked for a new feature, he was able to decide really fast. And he could make his decisions based on whether it was a big opportunity and he thought the business needed to win this. He could then get the new feature and commit to that customer. Markus and his team built a POC (proof of concept). Within a reasonable timeframe, the team was able to show the new feature to the customer before the customer made the final buying decision. That agility was necessary from the product features side of things to win deals. It is still today to some degree.

It all sounds basic, but it's not. And it's critical for businesses to get this point. It's particularly important when having no level of presence or any credentials in a market to be able to listen to customers' problems and needs, and to demonstrate that you have listened and taken into account their request. At the start of the journey in Europe, these really hard earned customers deserve your full attention. And your level of dedication to respond to their needs and your reliability in delivering is the key success factor to secure them. These early customers are critical; this is where success starts, one customer at a time. And the better you understand the needs of these first customers the faster you will understand and respond to 10 more customers with the same type of needs. It makes it much easier to scale, once you have done this deep dive into your European customers' needs. It sounds basic, but a lot of businesses want to shortcut this phase and want to see sales straight away. Unfortunately, it rarely happens. This is one of the reasons why the second attempt of Vigience worked. It was in-depth, methodical, and completely focused on the customer needs.

Customers

In terms of customers, their target market is quite well defined. Vigience's target customers are manufacturers that use SAP and Salesforce. Following SAP footsteps, Vigience initially started with the largest European companies and they are now targeting more mid-market companies to further expand their footprint.

In Japan, their end-customers are the top 50 manufacturers. However, **they are only approached through large, trusted advisors and not directly** (for example, Accenture, Deloitte). In Japan, the IT system integrators make the decision. Japanese customers outsource their solution architecture and decision-making process to global system integrators a lot more. So Japanese IT departments don't have strong opinions on technical matters. They contract big system integrators to do the background work and make proposals to them. These proposals are then accepted or rejected by the manufacturer. It means that the core evaluation of whether this is a good product or not is done by the global system integrator.

In Europe this is the opposite. Markus is present in most sales calls and he quickly realized that the European manufacturers have much stronger IT departments. These IT departments are much more involved in tactical decisions to buy from a vendor or not. They wouldn't leave that process to a system integrator. They're much more actively involved in the decision-making. So it's much more important for the Vigience team to convince the solution architect in the IT department of a manufacturer than the system integrator.

'In Europe, the customers' IT departments are much more involved in driving the decisions than in Japan. They are much more in control of what's going on, and that also changes how we sell and to whom. In Europe the customer is the decision marker, whereas in Japan the customers' trusted advisor, the system integrator, is the decision maker.'

That was a big shift for Vigience, and it changed their way of selling. These are the little things they are still fine tuning. As a consequence, in the marketing the message is addressed to the end-customer, the manufacturer, as a first priority.

> This is where a testing phase is a great way to get more insider information, before you start to allocate a huge amount of resources in people and marketing. You need to deeply understand who your audience is, otherwise you'll keep missing your target in your marketing, and you will guide your team towards the wrong direction. This is where market testing and gathering insider information are time and money savers. For Markus, knowing that his main target is not an intermediary (the system integrator) but the IT department of the manufacturer is a complete game changer.

In the initial stages of entering the European market for the second time, Markus, as the owner of the business, made a point to be in every customer call. Every sales meeting gave him additional information on whether the business was a good fit for the European customer. It enabled him to make decisions on the spot, to adjust and be agile.

Markus could take all these lessons from every sales call and make the relevant adjustments in his marketing efforts. When entering a new market, it's almost like starting from scratch, because you have different competitors, customers have different expectations and you have different customers.

Channel partners

In Europe for Vigience, the entry point at the beginning of the journey is the customer, then the channel partner. Whereas in Japan, because they do not have direct contact with large corporations, the entry point is the system integrators.

Initially, when Vigience entered the market, he could technically offer the customer either Microsoft or Salesforce as a CRM. In their second attempt to enter the European market, he decided to go with just Salesforce.

He committed the business to the Salesforce ecosystem. It was an important change. In the initial stages, not being focused on one partner made him and the team distracted. He was having a meeting with Microsoft Europe and then having another with Salesforce Europe. To really focus on one partner was key to success. Even though there may be times when it was easier to have meetings with Microsoft or there were opportunities, at the end of the day being focused on only one partner made them firmly established in one camp. It meant that Vigience was now part of the Salesforce ecosystem. The results are even better than with the dual-partner approach.

It allows Vigience to network much deeper in the channel partner sales organization.

So networking is now very focused, and also it allows training the team in a very focused way. They also know which marketing tool wins as well.

Having a focused approach to partners is really important for small teams to succeed. As Markus outlined, it can be distracting having too many salespersons to train, to pursue and to lobby. It takes a lot of time and it minimizes the impact – particularly when your partners are mammoth organizations like Microsoft and Salesforce with large sales teams. It can easily drain your resources. Instead, focusing on the right salespersons within one single organization produces better results. It makes it much easier to stay on top of their organization and also to get to know the high performers and the allies within the channel partners. This is very powerful.

'Vigience was entering the enterprise software market, where customers have long-established relationships with trusted advisors, such as their implementation partners, the system integrators or their long-term vendors. And the other thing with these customers is that they don't go and Google the Vigience solution. From the start, what we did right was to identify the system integrators that serviced our customers. We then started to chase them and just market our solution to them. Initially a few of them committed to Vigience. It's not like they said, "Okay, this is the best thing we've seen and I will go and sell this for you now." This is not how it works. Instead, if you do this long enough, you'll find they will make an introduction, they will show your product here or there. Then the first good opportunity comes in and you just grab it and pursue it. Then you make the system integrator partner look good and you make yourself look good. And there will be a follow-on project from there.'

From the start, Vigience did well with the channel partners by first focusing on their target customers' preferred ecosystem. It makes things happen faster. You do not have to convince a client that they have to use such-and-such channel partners; they save you time by telling you whom they have their contracts with. Then you just need to let the channel partner know *your customer wants to buy our product, let's work together on this deal.* Once you have a successful deal with this channel partner, this is when you showcase it to the channel partner sales team. You showcase how easy it is to deal with your organization, how they can easily add an extra line of revenue to their sales results by selling your product. You also outline how you and the team are going to provide support along the way. This is how partnerships achieve success for both parties.

How do you recognize a good channel partner? **According to Markus, a good channel partner gets what Vigience is.** They have understood the value that they provide and the difference between Vigience and the next closest competitor.

Once they understand this, it's 80% of the work the team must do.

Then the discussion is only about finding out if the solution is fit for the system integrator business problem and is the price acceptable or not. But then the hard work is how you position yourself, how you make people understand what is unique in what your business can offer. The more complex the product is, the harder it is to get that know-how out there.

Markus thinks they should put together a much better partner program: identifying the possible partners and then approach them. That is what they plan to do next.

A good channel partner brings the right deals to you, the ones that perfectly fit your capabilities. And I agree with Markus; this is when you know they have understood what your business offers. You will see that the fit is not quite right when a partner keeps trying to sell to the wrong target market at the wrong price point.

Country

In the case of Vigience, their sweet spot is countries with large manufacturing companies, who have a CRM for their sales teams and service processes and use SAP for their manufacturing, material management and warehouse management, and so on. Germany is a big manufacturing market. It also has a big SAP presence; almost everybody uses SAP there. Salesforce is gaining more and more traction, so that will be an interesting market for Vigience. The same thing with the UK, but Salesforce is a bit stronger there than Germany.

German-speaking markets are also big (DACH countries): Germany, Austria and Switzerland. Even though Switzerland is small, they are willing to pay high prices for something new and for quality.

Their best countries are Denmark, now, Germany, and then hopefully the next one is the UK. Denmark was the quickest adopter; it's a tech-savvy market. Switzerland is really hard, even if it is Markus's own country. Everybody knows everybody. Germany is quite open to newcomers.

Team

> 'The first time Vigience entered the European market, we
> spent a lot of money for our size. We had a team,
> we had a representative office. In retrospect, I think we
> were trying to enter the market by force. Vigience had
> more staff in Europe than we have now.'

As explained earlier, this is the second time they have tried to enter the market. Markus relates how they went about it the first time, and then how they are doing it now, the second time. The two approaches are completely different when it comes to human resources.

The first time Vigience entered the European market, they spent a lot of money for their size. In retrospect, Markus thinks they were trying to enter the market by force: they had a team, they had a representative office. They went to trade shows and hired dedicated companies to help with marketing and business development. It was an outsourced business development go to market.

Vigience had more staff in Europe than they have now. They had five to six full-time expensive employees in Switzerland. Markus reveals that they weren't able to break through. They obtained just a handful of customers. These early customers were invaluable. On the other hand, Markus comments that any professional investor wouldn't accept a performance like theirs at the time.

They found it a lot harder than initially thought. Markus thinks they underestimated it. Because he speaks the language and because he is a native of this region (Markus is Swiss), he thought it would be easier. But that isn't right, according to him.

The way they sell, the way they position themselves and the way they market is quite different in Europe versus Japan.

Markus also recognizes he made some mistakes that had nothing to do with the go to market strategy. He hired persons he knew already; they were 'friendlies' who left Japan because of Fukushima. He retrained them in specific new roles. The biggest difference is that the first time he had a person in place for each activity: one person would do the implementation side, someone else would do the demo, and then someone would do the sales side, negotiate and do the networking. He then hired an expensive marketing agency that would put together a marketing campaign. Then he hired external people to help with the go to market, which worked out almost to be the best. However, he realizes now that at the time he did not have a personal connection to the customer.

In hindsight, **he thinks they could not really get off the ground for multiple reasons: the people he hired didn't have experience in selling into this particular market, into this particular customer group, and they had no pre-existing connections**. Instead they were relying on some textbook processes: you do some lead genera-tion through some marketing activities and then the customers come to your website, fill in the contact form, then you do a demo. Markus realizes now that the whole thing just didn't work.

> What's important to note here as well is that Markus took over a leading sales role during the second attempt. And it is inter-esting to note that this was made possible as it was a global pandemic at the time and it was fully accepted to have meetings online. For this reason, he was able to attend all the sales meetings conducted online very easily.

I think the strategy to set up a subsidiary, set up teams and so on was not incorrect; the only issue was timing. It is only once you know precisely how to sell to the European customers that you should start staffing. This is how the second attempt was so much more successful. Markus knew precisely the customers' needs, and could build the team around these needs. It really does not work the other way around. This is why the second attempt, which was customer-centric, worked!

Marketing

'Now the second time around, we're going much leaner.
I did all of the messaging towards the market myself.
I mentally set the go-to-market and the messaging
for a new market. This was a CEO matter now.'

'The first time around we externalized the marketing function. We hired a marketing agency to put together PDF documents, we had the agency create the web presence and many other things, such as an online marketing campaign.

'Then the marketing company advised us to redo the website, so we started to do that. So everyone kept very busy, but nothing really happened. And it did not work at all.'

For the second attempt, Markus, the CEO, wrote every line of the marketing messages, the webpages and pamphlets. He went much leaner. He thought it was a bit crazy that he was writing this material. On the other hand, he realized he was the person who knew the product best, and every customer meeting and every sales meeting gave him additional information. It indicated where their product did not fit, or maybe it was their messaging, the way they presented, or the way they competed. He was able to take all these lessons from every sales call and adjust them into the marketing effort.

He thinks they are still in start-up mode. As soon as they have 30 to 50 customers, they will know the right prices, the message to the market, and the right partners for the go to market strategies. This is when he will start to step back.

Some of the things we ask for from our customers, in my business, when we start in Europe are a company profile, a value proposition and a product brochure, and we go from there. We may also need a slide deck. We do not need a lot of marketing collateral to start with, but the value proposition needs to be impactful. This is what matters. I understand why Markus felt he had to cut marketing right back, and to focus on refining and testing his value proposition and how this responds to his customers' needs. This is where marketing agencies sometimes fail – because they are not close enough to your customers, they don't always understand the message that is important to them. When you are a small business, you start with a focused approach on a limited number of profiles of your best target customers, and you create one message per profile tailored to them. That is all you need to create impact.

Dashboard

They are still at the start of their journey. Even though they are at their second attempt in Europe, they don't really have a sophisticated system to measure progress. They measure the number of deals they close. Markus thinks this is not enough, and as next steps they should probably measure 'if we have this amount of success, it means this is what works'.

At this stage in the business in Europe, they don't have a sales target. At the enterprise customer level, if they win a deal it's a lot of money, or on the other hand they could get it postponed for six months for reasons that have nothing to do with Vigience; for example, the customer experiences delays in their Salesforce or SAP implementation. So it's a bit of a challenge. Markus is not happy about that.

At this stage, he knows they don't have a repeatable and measurable business. Like SAP, their business is on the back of large corporates. So now like SAP as well, he has tried to diversify to more mid-market companies. That is why it's hard to plan and forecast right now. He thinks he will have to change that at some point. They need to have more mid-market deals to have shorter sales cycles (down from 12 months or more to six months), and also to have a larger volume of deals.

Markus is one of the few interviewees who was very clear on what they are currently doing around dashboards, targets and KPIs and how they track their sales. Given his corporate background and his line of business, he knows very well how customer relationship management software works. He knows what they need to do next in this field. This topic of measuring a pipeline of leads, sales conversions, and tracking against sales targets is a tricky one for smaller businesses. I personally love CRMs and I think there is so much that can be done with them. As a minimum, when you are a small business they can help your recordkeeping of past activities, and the management of opt-ins and opt-outs to comply with GDPR data protection obligations. Then you can build on their capability to create a sales pipeline, tracking the number of leads, conversions and so many other indicators.

But first and foremost, before getting lost and distracted in the system, it's important to know your customers, their needs and what and how you are going to sell to them. When you start to scale, then it's time to use a system.

* * *

TWO DIFFERENT PERSPECTIVES ON EXPORTING TO EUROPE

The next two export stories are quite different from the previous ones. I thought they would provide valuable perspectives with their two different ways to expand into the European market. The first approach is the one of Du-Co Ceramics, which brings a different way to enter the European market. Indeed, Du-Co has increased their footprint in the European market by way of acquisition of one of their long-standing American competitors, which had long-term customers in Europe.

The story of Ninja Beans is the second one that is slightly different to the others. I wanted to add it to the mix because it brings the perspective of a service business. This brings a different angle to this book, as it brings a fresh perspective on exporting.

Let me show you how both stories can add a string to your export bow.

Du-Co Ceramics: the case of acquisition to expand your European footprint

The story of Du-Co Ceramics is quite different in comparison to other companies in this book. First, it has a specific part that is designed for a specific use. It is well defined and identified, and international customers look for it and ask for quotes. This is why their Chairman, Tom Arbanas, mentioned during the interview that overall he feels they are not doing anything differently in Europe than what they are doing for their US customers.

Du-Co Ceramics are also working on breakthrough innovations exploring the many possibilities the ceramic material can offer. They have worked with NASA on specific projects, and they have also looked at environmental applications.

Du-Co Ceramics has historically developed their overseas customer base by attending international trade shows, such as Ceramitec in Germany. They have found that in Europe, customers – particularly Germans – are attracted by their high-quality products.

As they acquired a US competitor business they inherited brand new European customers. This involved some complexities. They also inherited a European sales agent network. On paper, both aspects sounded really appealing. It was a fast and nice extension to their business in Europe. However, what they found was not what they had anticipated. The level practiced with European customers was quite low, and needed to be renegotiated to return to profitable

Heating element manufacturers.	Custom-designed technical ceramics used in ignition systems of heating elements.	The German market has been their main European market.
They have no representative in Europe and look after worldwide enquiries with their customer service team, as well as their Vice-President for Sales.	Their website is their main marketing tool. Their customers use specific keywords when searching for Du-Co's product. Trade show exhibitions in Europe, such as Ceramitec, are key for Du-Co to meet their target customers.	They chose not to go through the path of setting up a distribution network as their product is custom-made. The distribution model does not work for Du-Co Ceramics.

How each company approached the European market

levels. And regarding the European sales agents, which sounded quite attractive on paper, Du-Co found out that their contracts were overly generous, bringing Du-Co to the decision to put an end to these contracts.[52]

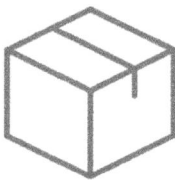

Product

Du-Co Ceramics is a manufacturer using one single material and process but it can produce a custom product every time. The process is typically as follows: the customer sends plans of the parts that they need, or sends samples. Then an estimating department will issue drawings based on what is provided and on what they can supply. Then the customer reviews the drawings. If the customer confirms this is the product they need, they pursue the quotation process. In essence, it means that the customer always gets a customized product. Overall, Tom highlighted the same materials and processes are used for all their customers globally. There might be slight variations in the types of parts, or the tooling could be different.

In the business of production and commercialization of technical ceramics, the price is very sensitive. Therefore, the euro versus US dollar exchange rate is an important indicator for Du-Co. Tom noted that quality was valued by Europeans. This has been very positive for them. Their great reputation for the quality of their products has helped in Europe, and particularly in Germany.

---

52 For US readers, a manufacturer's sales representative, paid most of the time on commission on sales only, is called a sales agent in Europe.

Customers

'After acquiring, they realized that some big accounts in Europe were priced at quite a low price. Du-Co corrected that over time.'

After they made the acquisition, a group of Du-Co managers traveled to Europe and visited many of the main customers that the company they acquired was doing business with. They also took the time to visit existing customers in several areas. They were primarily German customers. They were mainly companies making different types of electric heating elements.

They had been selling to customers in the United States similar types of ceramic products, so Du-Co is very knowledgeable and versed in that industry. They have pretty good knowledge of the type of companies that have a need for their exact type of product.

Their customers range from large household appliance names that are very well known to smaller heater manufacturers from different countries. They have about 1000 customers worldwide.

After the acquisition of the competitor business, they realized that some of their newly acquired big European accounts were priced quite low. They have had to correct that over time. The business they acquired was perhaps not charging enough for the products, and that might have been part of the reason they went out of business and Du-Co was able to acquire them.

On one hand, Du-Co was able to acquire extra customers, but on the other hand these customers were not profitable, given the price they bought the product at. It's a very delicate exercise to renegotiate pricing with customers you don't know. In the case of Du-Co, it meant they lost a few European customers along the way. Unfortunately, being in a price-sensitive market, the acquired business may have just won these European customers on price. This was not really adding any value to Du-Co.

Country

Du-Co inherited a lot of customers in Germany from the acquisition, and themselves had customers in Italy, France and Turkey. Since the pandemic, they are also doing business in Denmark, Switzerland, Poland and Ireland. These are small accounts.

As explained by Tom, the product is so clearly identified and their sales process so standard that they did not need to adapt any of their ways of doing business to Europe. This is very unusual, but is understandable in more mature industries such as the manufacturing of heating appliances. This is a well-established industry.

Channels

Du-Co Ceramics have never used distribution channels. They are selling directly to end-customers. On occasion they have sent out products to different locations via a distributor, but they do not see any benefit.

Because shipping costs play a big role in what they ship to Europe, they feel they just don't have enough business to entertain doing distribution over there. Each customer in Europe is buying multiple parts that are quite different. Many times that could be small quantities of different parts. That is probably why a distribution model would not be beneficial to them, with each product being customized for each customer.

Du-Co does not need any distributors in Europe, for several reasons. First of all, they get enquiries from manufacturers worldwide. They receive direct requests for quotations. The heating appliance manufacturers are used to ordering directly from their suppliers for this particular part. And on top of this, each part is custom designed to the customer's specifications. So distribution would not add a lot of value. A distributor would be needed if their product was a standard part, and if there were hundreds of customers per European country for Du-Co Ceramics. This is not the case and therefore does not justify the set up of a distributor.

Team

'The business we acquired did have representation over there. We chose not to maintain that relationship. We felt it was too expensive.'

Du-Co always goes direct and does not use distributors. However, the business they acquired had a network of independent reps, which was quite expensive. The financial arrangement included commissions, travel and office costs, and more. Du-Co decided not to maintain these relationships. They chose to use their own resources.

European sales agent contracts are quite standard. Each country usually has their own industry association that outlines the standard contractual arrangements that can be expected. They also often make available a standard agreement that can be used between a manufacturer and their sales agent. It's convenient to use these standard contracts because they can help you protect your business against unfair clauses. It also helps you understand your obligations and comply with them. It's always better to know in advance how to stop a contract if things don't work out, and what the process is. There are often notice periods, and indemnities that need to be calculated. Another way to protect your business is to make sure you are not the only business your sales agent represents, otherwise by law they can ask you to pay some extra social benefits. There could also be taxes related to this newly qualified 'employment', and it can be retroactive. So, check the local obligations before you sign up sales agents.

On the Du-Co side, the arrangement they inherited was quite unusual, as they had to pay for all the agents' expenses, in addition to commissions. This is not a great arrangement. The standard approach is to only have a commission on sales. Some manufacturers may accept some subsidies in the initial months as they get started, but definitely not long term.

Normally sales agents work best when they already know your customers and already visit them for other products, and your product is just an additional one they are going to sell to them.

On paper, having people in Europe sounded like a great opportunity, but this arrangement was not viable.

'If you speak two languages you're bilingual, if you speak one language you're American.' This is a joke that Tom shared with me. **Tom and the US-based sales team made trips to visit customers throughout Europe after the acquisition** (about five times over seven years). A lot of people spoke English, but Tom thought that it was always better to have an interpreter.

They organized themselves to have multiple contacts in the business looking after these European customers. They have very high marks for their customer service, based on surveys. Their Vice President of Sales is in contact with European customers quite frequently and has been for over 10 years. He has a background in the ceramics industry, of around 30 years. They have the same level of experience with their Vice President of Marketing, who has been with Du-Co for about 15 years. He also communicates with European customers on a regular basis. He also has a very long background in selling ceramics going back 30 years.

Marketing

They have looked for European customers in the past by attending European trade fairs and occasionally visited the market.

Because they have a deep understanding of the profile of companies that need their exact product, they have been able to use their website as a real magnet for international leads. They think it has helped them a great deal to secure more accounts.

They were planning to be present at major shows in 2021, namely Ceramitec and Hannover Messe. When they exhibit at shows their aim is to attract customers. They try to see most of their existing customers too, and if unable to meet them at the show they will visit them.

The acquisition opened some new opportunities for the business that were initially hard to leverage, given some of the 'fixing' that the Du-Co Ceramics team had to do. To keep sales at their current level, a yearly visit from a senior sales manager and the excellent customer service that they currently provide will help to maintain customer loyalty. When things get a bit tougher pricewise, and when the competition gets more intense, I think it adds a lot of value to be a bit more on the front foot to protect your market position. For example, as the Du-Co team have plans to exhibit at Hannover Messe and Ceramitec at the time of the interview, I would use both opportunities to meet the combined customer base of the two companies. I would survey these customers to understand where they go to look for ceramic products and also what Du-Co could do to work with them again. I would also work on developing a comprehensive mapping of potential European targets, focused on the traditional core customer base of heating appliances, but also looking at potential new targets based on the successful new innovative projects conducted in other industries in the US. With this mapping in hand, I would check if I am already in contact with these companies, or if despite the extension provided by the acquisition I have not reached out to all the major European players. To target new industry verticals, shows like Hannover Messe are great because a diverse range of industries visit to source equipment.

Tom was quite generous in reflecting on the acquisition. Their business decision was not motivated by the acquisition of new customers in Europe. But I believe that this is a valid strategy to expand into Europe. One of the ways that could be considered is to acquire a business in Europe or a business in your home country that has already done some great work in their international expansion. However, some lessons were learnt along the way, and you will learn more in the lesson part of this book.

Bean Ninjas: the fluidity of a 100% digitally operated business

Bean Ninjas has a completely different profile to the other case studies in this book. This is a service business, operated 100% online. This is quite a unique approach to business. I think it has quite a lot of value for manufacturers and software businesses to read this case study, even if it feels quite remote. There is a lot to learn from digitally savvy businesses when you are not!

As a business founded by digital nomads for digital nomads, Bean Ninjas has a completely different take on expanding overseas than traditional businesses. The location of the teams is not that important. Tom relocated to the UK from Australia, where he became a partner of Bean Ninjas and responsible for the development of the European business. Initially he kept his North American clients to fund his profit center while he built the UK market. In doing so he also built a team in Serbia to grow his delivery capability. This way he could grow his customer base in the UK and is able to service more customers. As he has built systems and processes for his service delivery team, he is now able to focus on growing the business and is less focused on operations.

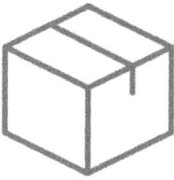

Product

Bean Ninjas offer bookkeeping services that are delivered exclusively online. Their target market is e-commerce businesses. They have a deep understanding of online marketplaces and they know how to navigate these online platforms. Their knowhow is so unique that very large accounting firms tend to refer customers to them. It's quite different from traditional bookkeeping as the figures come from a lot of different places. It is not just one bank account! It's a lot more complicated. Bean Ninjas are very familiar with platforms such as PayPal, and how these types of platforms integrate. They know how to balance them and to feed them into a traditional accounting system.

To simplify the business, they have stayed away from tax or anything that is country specific.

E-commerce businesses using multichannel sales.	Bookkeeping service.	UK specific for now. However, the UK entity is also servicing North American businesses.
The Australian HQ has appointed a UK-based partner, Tom, to look after the UK market. Tom has set up a Serbia-based service delivery team to support him in the delivery.	So far quite limited. It has not been a big focus.	A channel strategy is to be developed. The focus is to develop a partnership with Xero.

How each company approached the European market

A flexible service contract with no fixed term has been a key to their success. The pricing model is to pay in advance for the month. They have quite a flexible package system; customers can upgrade and downgrade as well. So customers are comfortable signing up. It's not like they have to commit for 12 months upfront.

They had to adapt their services. In the UK and in Europe, they have the bookkeeping and accounting provided by the same service provider and not separated. It required some adjustments in comparison to servicing Australian or US customers.

The value proposition is quite well articulated. And the business model is deliberately lean and simple. Anything that could be country specific is not catered for. It simplifies the organization and the service delivery. It also minimizes risk for the business. Accounting firms providing tax advice need to be knowledgeable about the local tax system and keep up to speed with local tax changes. Imagine for a small business what effort it would take to learn every single European tax system and stay constantly up to date with them – that would require a tremendous amount of time and skill, and this would be very hard to keep up with for a small team. So I found it quite interesting that to get a fast start, Tom decided to go with a non-specific service.

Customers

'Reputation building was key.'

When Tom started they had about 20 to 30 clients. Now they have about 60. They doubled in just under a year. They have been successful with e-commerce firms because they are able to provide them with simple views on the profit per product or per region they are selling to. They can see where they are successful. They can detect if cash dropped in a specific market. Or can show which European country gets bigger profit margins. Providing these types of figures to e-commerce firms is so valuable that most of their business grew through word of mouth. They didn't start any paid marketing campaigns for about four years, and before that was organic growth. So reputation building was key.

Again the target customers are unique and have unique needs; they are firms selling on e-commerce. It simplifies the value proposition. Also the provision of the service online to this type of customer is completely aligned with the e-commerce businesses being very accustomed to running online.

Country

Bringing on Tom was the strategy to look after the UK and grow the customer base there. They are very focused on the UK for now. They have an international base, but Tom is focusing more on UK-specific things now. They have a few customers in Denmark.

However, Tom's view is given the size of the three main markets of the UK, France and Germany, the other markets will be much smaller. So he does not think it is worth the effort focusing on the other countries first.

> Again, the focus on the UK first, where he is setting up the initial revenue base before branching out to new European countries, is wise. This allows him to provide a great service level, grow revenue and validate his strategy before expanding to a new country, where he might still have to adapt his approach.

Channels

Partnership with large accounting firm Xero is a key strategy that Tom is pursuing, which means getting to know the right persons within their organization and their partner network. The business only works with Xero so it makes quite a natural partner for them. Tom is focusing on building a chain of connections. Xero personnel need to know what Bean Ninjas does, and so do Xero partners.

> Again, focusing on one single partner and building the ecosystem around it is very wise. The partner might not be the same in the next two European countries. For example, Xero is not available in France and Germany for now. So a different local partner, well-established in the local e-commerce world, would be wise. A focus partner per country is generally a good way to go in Europe. Pan-European channel partners are not always easy to find, and if you dig a little deeper you often find they are not performing well in every single country.

Team

> *'The service delivery team does not own one big customer, they all have a small section of the projects that each of them focuses on. This way they can adapt and change very quickly to the environment around them.'*

Bean Ninjas' original customers are mainly digital nomads who move around the globe. It means that having cloud-accountants based in the Philippines and the head office in Gold Coast Australia was very suitable to their digital tribe of customers. It means they would always be able to be serviced by someone in their time zone.

Tom was quite aligned with the business. He was looking for an online bookkeeping business that would enable him to live anywhere and sustain a living. Tom purchased the European side of the business and now focuses on the European expansion.

Tom is still very involved in the day-to-day business. But he has built a service delivery team based in Serbia. He has established a supervisor, who is his right hand, and they have two cloud accountants as well.

The service delivery team does not own one big customer, they all have a small section of the projects that each of them focuses on. This way they can adapt and change very quickly to the environment around them. This is also a key attribute to their organization that differentiates them from very large and inflexible accounting firms, which are slower and clunkier in their approach.

Tom Mercer also learned that **as the business grows, separating the management and having clear lines of command is very important**.

I think everyone has to learn from the digital nomad approach. Of course, a manufacturer cannot go 100% digital; it still needs to produce physical goods, and have R&D and technical teams collaborate face to face, and develop prototypes. We all understand that. But the fluidity of a global team that operates fully digitally is an interesting asset. For example, Tom mentioned that at the start of the business in the UK, because he spoke Spanish he was still servicing a few Mexican customers. This allowed him to fund his UK-based entity, along with other US companies he was servicing too. In parallel he started to build the UK business. Building teams in a different time zone (UK, then Serbia) is of course adding a cost center but it also gives some extra resources for other time zones to tap into. Then as the European business builds up the team can be better leveraged to service their own time zone. It's a smart way to move into Europe.

Another interesting take away from Tom was the time he spent working on procedures for his team to become quickly autonomous to free his time. This is something that we commonly see in a service business.

Marketing

They haven't really done much in terms of UK and European specific marketing yet. Tom is looking forward to getting started. Events will mainly be where they will market. They have active communities online and also circles (for example, Dynamite Circle) and online groups that regularly meet up in an international location. He acquired two UK-based clients from this gathering in the past.

Writing blog articles that are more specific to the UK is also part of his marketing strategy. He is also offering entry-level services such as health checks and free trials to sign up new customers.

Tom is now looking at funding his European activities via new UK customer acquisitions.

It's interesting again to note that digital businesses think straight away about building communities online. And this is often overlooked by other industries. In addition, building online content such as specific blog articles about a specific topic is not always the preferred marketing strategy of manu-facturers, whereas digitally operated businesses, including software and service businesses, have a strong focus on online presence through content. This is often overlooked. I remember talking to team members of the Australian unicorn Atlassian and one of their core strategies from day one was creating content online that was curated to their audience. This is what allowed them to be found by their highly digitally educated customers (software developers would search everything online, of course!). This is an import-ant point, as in our post-pandemic era, Europeans are more connected than ever. And they search for information about their future purchases online.

Dashboard

They do automation as much as they can. They use a lead platform to manage the number of leads and number of calls coming in. For that they also get marketing reports from Google business.

Chapter 6

Challenges

Nothing like a good challenge to trigger and implement changes in a business. The companies interviewed have generously shared their challenges in the process of exporting to Europe, and how they have solved them. I think this is very commendable. I feel very privileged, and I take it as a gift that the interviewees have kindly shared them for the benefit of you, the reader, who are most probably in the process of beginning exporting or are already exporting.

Phoenix challenges: lighter product design and better packaging for more cost-effective shipping and better product integrity at delivery

One of the challenges that Vinod mentioned was packing. They had to solve this challenge pretty quickly by getting packaging experts to come in and improve this side of the operation. They realized that poor packing of their unit resulted in damaged products arriving at the other side of the world. This ruins a lot of efforts.

In addition, they have had to solve the issue of the weight of their product. Phoenix's European customers and partners mentioned that they really found the equipment fantastic, but why did they use material that was so heavy like iron, while there were other materials that were lighter? By making it lighter, the customers would find it easier to move around. And quite importantly, the cost of freight was high. As Vinod mentioned, 'If you have a product worth $100 and the customer has to spend $150 on freight, it does not make any business sense.' So they implemented this change in the product.

> Exporting forces you to look at your product with different lenses. Here is an ever-increasing challenge that every manufacturer has to take into account at conception of the product. The packaging is important to make sure it's delivered without any damage, but another factor to take into account is the sustainability of your packaging. Remember from part I of this book how Europeans value sustainability? More sustainable packaging, besides its overall positive impact, will also help your European distributors or customers meet their sustainability goals. Minimizing freight costs and taking into account the sustainability impact of your product at its design phase are much easier to manage than down the track.

Bean Ninjas challenges: funding European market expansion

Tom Mercer talks about the challenges of funding the European expansion. Tom is based in the UK, and he had a few British clients quite rapidly in his niche target market that is e-commerce. And initially, they were able to capture a few more clients organically. However, he still had to subsidize his entity by maintaining the US customers he was looking after that were not e-commerce. And that gave him a bigger business base. He started by subsidizing his European business development with a few large US customers.

When Tom compares his sales process with US clients and with Europeans, he feels that the sales cycle is much longer in Europe than in the US. He happened to have signed some American customers on a first call, while it systematically takes him several sales calls for their Europeans to sign up: first he talks to them, then they go away and have a think about it, then they come back for another call. He feels the mindset is a bit different, so he has to be a bit more patient and provide a lot more information.

Of course, Tom being based in the UK and being in the accounting and bookkeeping business, it has been very turbulent due to Brexit being implemented and also due to the changes in the Value Added Tax (VAT) rules for e-commerce in Europe. As of July 1, 2021, the Import One-Stop Shop (IOSS) system has been implemented.[53] Tom explains that basically when products are imported into different European countries, you have to account for the VAT rate that is in place in the customer's country. So there has been a lot more regulation in e-commerce he has had to adapt the business processes to.

Funding entering new international markets is always a challenge for any business. Whatever the size of the business, you have to invest time and effort and allocate a budget to make it work. Ideally your 'normal' business allows you to fund this expansion. When going to the European market, one of the key aspects is persistence. This is something that is very specific to the European way of doing business; you have to demonstrate that your business is there for the long term before European customers trust you and your business. It means that businesses with limited resources that are not able to sustain a year or sometimes two without significant

---

53 The Import One-Stop Shop (IOSS) is the electronic portal businesses have been able to use since July 1, 2021 to comply with their VAT e-commerce obligations on sales of imported goods.

revenue generated will not reap the benefits of their initial investment. Big business comes in time. European customers are generally loyal if your solution works for them. In the early stages of my business at Exportia, I made the mistake to take to Europe businesses that were too early stage and did not have the funds to persist in Europe. We would typically conduct a project over three to six months, get initial traction, but no solid deals yet. So they would decide to stop their European endeavor and try another market! Six months later the multinational I had contacted on their behalf contacted me to see if we could do something. What a frustration – we know that there is early positive feedback that will turn into sales in the coming months, and we have to stop the project! So to Tom's point, it's better to be in a financial position to allow a continuous and consistent effort. And yes, it's true, European customers may take time to convert, but medium to long-term effort pays off.

CleanSpace challenges: where do you hire in Europe?

The language was not really a challenge, it was more about demonstrating that you have your feet on the ground. Often customers ring you or email you and you have a short window where they are thinking about your brand. They have the brand for five minutes in their heads and then they move on to something else, as they are busy people. So it's critical to have people there, but you cannot organize that straight away. When you start in Europe you don't know where your customers are going to be, so where do you hire? Dr Birrell mentions that the difficulty initially is to know which language or country you are going to get the most traction in. So they quickly realized that they needed to invest as a business in Europe before they started to hire. They realized they needed to spend some time getting to know the market. They did not know initially if the market would be in the UK, France, Germany or the Nordics, for example.

> I am so grateful that Alex brought this challenge up. I think this is a very common dilemma for non-European businesses: where to go first? And if you can recall Joe brought it up as well. Indeed, a critical key success factor in Europe is to start in the right country and to have the right person in the right country!

Du-Co challenges: keeping customers after an acquisition

Some of the challenges that Du-Co Ceramics faced in Europe were mainly due to the acquisition. Over a period, Tom mentioned that they seemed to have lost some of the big business that was brought to them through the acquisition. At the time, the European customers explained that the new increased price level, in addition to the import tariffs and freight, were the key contributing factors.

Tom recognizes that what enabled them to afford to acquire their competitor was the fact that the competitor underpriced. So when they had to revisit the pricing structure of these newly acquired European customers, they had no choice but to increase their pricing. It resulted in losing a few.

> Inheriting European customers with the acquisition was quite attractive at the time, but the transition to Du-Co stand-ards did not allow Du-Co to keep them long term. It may

have been for the best. Customers that do not pay for your products at the right price end up not being worth keeping. These are hard decisions to make. And transitioning customers through acquisition is a delicate matter; you may not have all the information about these customers before you acquire a business to really know what they are worth before you buy.

Fluxergy challenges: being in start-up mode when you come from a corporate background

Dr Ali Tinazli noticed that it was a fun challenge for him personally. Moving from corporate to start-up world means for example that you will not always get a response to your emails! Dr Tinazli previously worked at Sanofi, Thermo Fisher and HP, and these are strong email domain names. It was quite an interesting learning curve. He also noted that things take longer than you anticipate when you enter a new market; patience is key.

Dr Tinazli also expressed the challenge of a technology-oriented company. It has a 'nerdy' side that sometimes may overpower the business side and may be an impediment to having a deeper connection to the clinical world and a deeper grounding in the clinical problem statements.

Dr Tinazli also shares that while shipping from California to Europe, the packaging needs to guarantee that the product keeps working when it lands in Europe. The other side is to ensure products are not stuck in customs, that the shipping time is not too long, and shipping is not too expensive while at the same time not forgetting that in Europe you need a euro plug!

Some of the challenges that are specific to Europe are because it is a highly fragmented market. For example, Dr Tinazli observes that even if they share languages, Austrians and Germans have a different mentality.

In addition, in the line of business of Fluxergy, there might be additional local authorizations needed in each country beyond the Europe-wide compliance CE mark (in Fluxergy's case, CE-IVD). He finds that a local distribution partner is often helpful to overcome this challenge.

One of the interesting challenges, that I particularly noted, was the one of transitioning from the corporate world to start-up mode. This is one that Markus from Vigience mentioned as well. In my experience at Exportia, we have had to deal with different types of professionals; some came from corporate, others from small business, others did not have any business background and were engineers, scientists or medical professionals. Generally speaking, the attitude, the motivation, the willingness to start from scratch and being open to learn and be agile are key attributes to succeed in a market where your business is a completely unknown entity. As Dr Tinazli mentioned, it means that even if you are a senior professional with a stellar corporate background, showing persistence, rolling up your sleeves to reach customers and understanding their needs like Markus Stierli and Dr Tinazli did is the first step to success in any European country. They both have been flexible enough to adapt to this brand-new world – the hard work had to be done. There is no bypassing this phase at the start. I too worked in corporate, and I can recognize a lot of value in a corporate experience in so many ways, like in setting-up systems, structuring teams, in the ways to work or not with distributors. So there is a lot of positive to that too.

Challenges

Futramed challenges: reintroducing a technology that was never heavily adopted in the past

The main challenge for Matt was to reintroduce a technology that was never heavily adopted in the past. Being able to get any kind of track record with their technology in the field validated is a challenge, and that's something they have just started. This was their challenge at the time of the interview, with six-month product trials. Doing the initial field testing was a challenge. It was mainly for them to make sure they had a working prototype.

The CE marking process has taken a long time, since they were on a budget. But they made it successfully.

In the medtech sector, providing clinical evaluation is critical to being able to sell and to convince potential customers. This is part of the process and requires working very closely with medical key opinion leaders in their specialty; getting them to test the product and write about it is the goal. When it comes to achieving compliance in the European market, it has been a challenge lately in the medtech sector as the requirements have become more stringent. It has been a steep learning for some businesses, with the level of quality management systems required. There are also new types of medical products that from now on fit into the new regulations (such as software, and aesthetics prosthetics). Some have also changed risk class. It has meant quite a lot of changes in the requirements to be compliant with this medical device regulation.

Generally speaking, when complying with European norms, specifically for a CE mark for your product, many of you would already be aware that non-European businesses need to meet specific requirements, if you do not have an entity registered in one of the European member states.

The European Union issued in June 2019 a further extension to its regulatory requirements.[54] In essence, this new regulation applies to a long list of directives for a large number of products. All the directives that this new regulatory requirement applies to are listed in this directive. There are 70 directives listed.

Joe L. challenges: it's always easy to assume that one culture understands another

Joe L. shared that a lot of the time, challenges are cultural. He thinks it's always easy to assume that one culture understands another. However, from a sales perspective, people still buy from people, no matter how good the technology is. As the business Joe works for was in a position of being evangelistic – in other words, there weren't a lot of companies around the world doing what they were doing – the people they were selling to had to be big thinkers. Joe says they are not a mainstream software provider so they *had* to be evangelical in a way. You're trying to convince people they need something that they didn't know existed until they found out about you. So the idea of connecting culturally and using local networks was really when things started to change for them.

Challenges

---

54 Regulation (EU) 2019/1020 of the European Parliament and of the Council of July 20, 2019 on market surveillance and compliance of products. https://eur-lex.europa.eu/legal-content/EN/TXT/?uri=CELEX%3A32019R1020.

I think the comment on the cultural challenge complements the remarks of Dr Ali Tinazli and Markus Stierli around having to go back to basics and sell when you enter the market. However, they both did not have cultural barriers to overcome in Germany as they are both German native speakers, but they still found it a challenge to do the initial sales. So imagine having no German skills at all and trying to sell a breakthrough technology where you have to be evangelical, like Joe and his team had to be, with no local language skills. This is why it is crucial to get some local support from native speakers as soon as you have validated the country you would like to focus on, and where you have gained initial traction. Only that deeper cultural connection and understanding will allow you to make it.

Vigience challenges: perception of a start-up in Europe

Some of the challenges that Markus highlighted are based on his experiences with the US and Europe. Vigience is still at start-up stage. In the US, this is seen as a competitive advantage, because you're innovative and new. In Europe, a start-up is perceived as a risk! You have that challenge that Europeans will only buy from established players. In the US, nobody looks down on you because you're a start-up – they see there's an opportunity. It's not the case in Europe.

There are differences in communication style too. In the US, you can move in quickly but you might be out quickly as well. Whereas in Europe, you make relationships that survive months and years, and you can stay in touch, which Markus found harder to do in the US.

These comparisons between the US market and the European market are very insightful for readers from the US and also from other nations. If you are at an early stage, you indeed are going to have to demonstrate your credentials to potential European buyers. When we work with early-stage companies in Europe – and as it happens we have one in our portfolio right now – and our targets are government organizations or corporations in France, Germany and Switzerland, the way we achieve our first sales is to use the government and corporate contracts they had in their domestic market. As Joe mentioned, he used his American corporate footprint, and the American businesses opened the doors to them in their European subsidiaries.

In short, when you are an early-stage business, you have to use whatever credentials you currently hold in your domestic market or anywhere else overseas, as long as the references can carry some weight in the eyes of your European buyer.

Another challenge being a Japanese company, even though Markus is a Swiss citizen, was that he is of the opinion that emotionally there is no way a European customer would have bought from a Japanese entity. Emotionally, it's two different worlds. A European business can buy from California, for example, but they would never buy from a Japanese entity. This is why early on Markus had set up a European entity to quote an invoice from, specifically for European customers.

That comment is also interesting. I think from Markus's perspective he was thinking about European corporates that would not be comfortable buying direct from Japan. There are ways around this. Of course, the way that Vigience has counteracted this is by setting up an entity. This is one way. The downside to a new entity is that it can be costly, and at the start you may not be 100% sure where the best location would be for your entity.

There is an alternative to a new entity to make it easy for your European customer to buy from you: they can buy your product or solution from your local channel partner or distributor. This is very common, and it is a very efficient way to get a market started. It's flexible and it gives you time to evaluate where to set up an entity and hire. Plus a channel partner strategy can be a long-term one.

In addition, it was also a challenge for Markus and his team at Vigience that in their domestic market in Japan, the end-customer does not get involved in the initial product selection process. Japanese customers have outsourced this function to a business that I called in the IT industry a system integrator. In Japan, the end-user of the enterprise software is not involved in this part of the process. In Europe, the IT departments are completely involved in the process. This means that Markus had to completely rethink their pitch and their sales process and adjust them in order to pitch, develop marketing collateral for and sell to end-users.

The use of trusted intermediaries in Japan is a very common practice; that is not the case in Europe. Typically, in my business, we strongly recommend to any business entering the European market that they talk to the end-users of the product, even if they are working with distributors. I am even an advocate of continuous direct contact with your European customers. It's important to stay independent from channel partners, because sometimes they perform well and at other times they don't, and it gives you the ability to shift and change your distribution strategy to make sure you reach your revenue targets. In addition, keeping close contact with European customers enables you to stay in tune with the European customers' needs. You can learn from them, and it can be so helpful when launching a new product – you can then easily get early market feedback from them. My experience is that end-users will value these direct contacts with you and it does make them loyal; they love giving feedback and sharing what they and their industry need. In addition, I find that most European distributors appreciate the support of the vendor or from the manufacturer; it shows their customers that you support them. Visits to end-users together with your channel partner or your local distributor are a great way to show support. Another aspect that I find valuable is the fact that if any distributor if not doing the right thing with your product, the end-customer can always reach out to you if they know you. It's a great safety net.

Chapter 7

Successes

In my experience, successes in the European market can take many forms and shapes.

It is often about winning a large deal, but what matters is finding the right recipe that will enable your organization to succeed in a consistent manner. As I interviewed these businesses, I was looking for a mechanism that they found helped them build success rather than a list of achievements and victories. I think these recipes for success are great takeaways for any exporters.

CleanSpace successes: navigating across languages, building a distribution network and a European customer base of large corporates

Let's start with Dr Alex Birrell from CleanSpace, where she explains how they successfully built a European network of distributors, and how they used their first wins with large European corporate accounts. She also explains how they smoothly navigated multilingualism.

They had no issue with languages with partners and agents. They were able to use Google translate, and particularly with partners like Exportia we could overcome the language barrier.

In America, they are looking for Americans so that was one of their challenges, getting somebody on the ground in the US.

The CEO says that once they had done Australia and they were working in Europe, they were able to use these experiences and learnings in the North American market. They knew the type of distributors and customers. They already had built key reference sites. They knew the types of shows and marketing tools that enable you to get the brand out there.

CleanSpace embraced the European way of doing business, and they were fast to adjust to a multilingual environment. Their specialists were always supportive and would regularly jump on the plane to conduct customer visits with us when we needed them. It meant that CleanSpace management developed a great insider understanding of the market. It really helped to accelerate success and get fast results. It's interesting to note that CleanSpace found that a lot of their learnings they could take with them to the US market. I personally think that Europe is a great testing market for other parts of the world; it's diverse culturally, it's a place where businesses discover how to embrace multilingualism, they can scale to a varied range of industries. European customers don't judge very well companies that don't provide what they need in their languages. For example, distributors just won't push your brand if they cannot share with their sales teams brochures in their own language. CleanSpace thrived on this aspect, and from the European customer perspective you come one step closer to them if you make that effort.

Distribution is something where CleanSpace has done well, thanks to its key ability to pivot and learn from mistakes and being able

Successes

to adjust accordingly. Every company has its own personality, and they are just like any other business. Distributors have growth phases, changes in management, changes in strategy. They might be doing a merger or an acquisition which might distract them. Sometimes, you start working with them, they are not successful and then they become successful and with other partners, or they are successful in the first few years, then something happens like a corporate restructure and they take their eyes off the ball. So it's never 'set and forget' with distribution.

When they work with distributors, they are always looking for the right partner and looking to understand what's motivating them, what's distracting them and what is coming up in their business that may impact their sales? And they are looking at what could help accelerate the sales with this partnership.

The key for CleanSpace according to the CEO was to be quick to learn from their mistakes and pivot and adjust accordingly. When they pick a distributor, they start by mapping the distribution channels and then work out what's best for their business now, and that may change over time as well. And the channels themselves may change too. Being agile is important.

As they were new to the European market, Dr Birrell realizes that initially they were not active enough in investigating the distribution channels as well as they would have liked. And they were not active enough in partnering and driving the partnerships. She realizes it was understandable as they were new to the market and did not know what they did not know. So moving forward they were successful because they did a lot of research and investigation on distribution, and were quite active in the way they set partnerships up and managed them on an ongoing basis. Any company doing that for the first time has to be prepared to fail, learn and adjust.

For companies entering the European market, at Exportia we usually recommend setting up distribution one country at a time. To be able to do that, we usually conduct a market validation phase, which involves choosing the top two countries which not only are the best markets for that business but also have an appetite for it right now. Mapping out the landscape should really be a prerequisite for anyone wanting to set up distribution. Too many businesses I have seen over the years skip this step and they end up spending a lot of years stuck with an underperforming distributor. And I often notice these businesses don't have a clear map of the distributors out there. More often than not, they have just appointed a distributor that has come to them. This is clearly not what happened with CleanSpace – they did thorough research of the distribution landscape and it paid off.

The fact that distribution is never set and forget is so true! Distributors are indeed their own business and they have their own priorities. You constantly need to make sure you stay part of their priorities and that they stay motivated to continue selling for you. It's particularly important for distributors that may distribute your brand alongside a competitor's brand; you really have to work hard on building your allies and your brand supporters inside the distributor's organization to make it work long term. We call these allies your sales champions inside the organization. Vinod from Phoenix also mentioned his emphasis on key sellers within the distributors; he usually even builds a motivation plan just for them.

Dr Birrell attributes the success of CleanSpace with large corporate accounts to a lot of hard work, market research and trying to find low-hanging fruit. Learning from other markets where you have been successful and identifying similar companies that have similar operations is valuable. That's where research comes in. It's about working out the best way in and getting an introduction to these companies. That might be your traditional marketing programs, lead generation or trade show advertising – all these activities can enable you to get in-bound leads from these companies.

In addition, the distributors are important for getting traction with key accounts, as you can put pressure on them to help you access some of the larger sites and they can do an introduction. These large corporate accounts have safety days, and that's where CleanSpace is able to demonstrate their product.

That's some of the key actions they have been successful with. At the end of the day, it comes down to persistence: you may come in the front door or from five different ways to try to find the right people and the right stakeholders for you.

Even sometimes after 20 phone calls and still hearing no, no, no, you just have to keep working the system as best as you can to get to the right people. It's not just about one reference site; these large corporate accounts have multiple operations, so you're trying to find that first site that's going to give you a foot in the door so that you can start to work your way through.

That is what Dr Birrell calls their 'land and expand' model. Maybe even just a small deployment or a small sale via one site would give the opportunity to try to work through to get a bigger deployment on that site, and then maybe go site to site. It's about getting a referral to the next site, then talking at the corporate level. But the first 'landing' into that first site has been a major recipe for success for CleanSpace to then enable further expansion.

In my business, we call this finding the 'anchor customers'. CleanSpace did really well to build a customer base of European multinationals. It takes a lot of time and attention to make sure you are closing rapidly your first European corporate clients, and that you look after them really well to make sure they become your advocates in the market. They are critical to your success, as these customers enable you to establish credibility in the market, particularly when you are a newcomer. When a large European player is adopting your technology as their best practice, that is often when they even go a step further and start to advocate their best practice within their industry. Within an anchor client (the large corporation) they will have key opinion leaders who are well respected within their organization, and often it goes that they also have a voice in their industry. So they deserve your full attention.

Futramed successes: building a network of French doctors that were able to provide very useful early feedback

The best path for Futramed was to build a network of French doctors. Matt Harding started with a very good introduction to a highly influential doctor. It really helped at the start. Matt has an atypical profile, as he had been a professional musician for 30 years. In that way, he believes he has been very successful in using his strength in building deep relationships with the doctors he meets. He realizes this is not the typical way Americans approach business, and that has been really successful so far for them to be able to rely on these doctors' feedback.

In addition, what was really helpful was Matt's experience traveling the world; by the time he started working for Futramed, he had a great deal of international experience. He had gone through some very uncomfortable realizations. Matt mentioned that he was able to realize that there were a lot of things he was doing reflexively, based on his American background, that were absolutely wrong. On these occasions, he experienced how one can make a fool of oneself.

So he is now extremely culturally sensitive. Being an American business worked in their favor, as Matt's profile and cultural sensitivity actually acted against a negative stereotype.

> Matt's interpersonal skills and cultural sensitivity have certainly contributed immensely to connecting with French doctors. They were able to make meaningful inroads into this market because they were very open to listening, trying to understand, taking the time, and they were culturally flexible. Humility always pays off.

Joe L. successes: in the business of numbers

On successes, Joe takes it down to the fact that they are in the business of numbers. And there is an international language of numbers – as a software company they are giving insights on data. So the good thing for the business is that data does not lie.

Joe has found Europe a different culture all together – the way things are negotiated and the way things are handled – but that's really why he thinks they were able to penetrate the European market fairly easily: in their case he says it really all does come down to numbers!

> I think Joe is modest here. It does not all come down to numbers. The business he works for has been very persistent and consistent in the market. They have adapted their approach over the years. I personally think that besides

the excellence of their product, their commitment to the European market was their key to success.

Phoenix successes: differentiated product design

Their differentiated product design was one of their biggest successes. They **invested heavily in creating their very differently shaped baby warmer**, which is in a beautiful oval shape. It is according to Vinod their biggest success point.

Another key point of success for them was to successfully partner with European companies to ultimately reach one of their large target markets, Africa. As soon as they signed an OEM deal with a Swiss company, they were able to win these types of deals. That enabled them to sell to UNICEF through an agreement with a German business. This was a successful strategy.

Vinod thinks what made him and the business successful was also **his systematic approach to sales**. As he describes it, he kept grinding and grinding, and kept in touch until they tried his unit out. By being consistent, he saw a shift appearing. Initially, European businesses do not recognize that you are a player. And then, they will start recognizing you as a player if you put in the work and stick around. Even if they did not win the business, Vinod would keep in touch with them continuously – he would keep sending them product information and offers.

One interesting success story that Vinod shared was also a turning point in his career. Vinod went to Copenhagen to present to UNICEF and advocate for the adoption of the use of LEDs instead of 15-year-old technologies that were still used. Vinod presented and advocated for the adoption of lower-power-consumption LEDs to health development experts. LEDs had been a proven technology for years, which the world was massively adopting – why was UNICEF lagging?

When he later found out that LED technology was being adopted in the UNICEF specifications, Vinod felt a huge increase of confidence and pride, as he was not only talking for his company but for the industry as a whole and for the benefit of babies worldwide. It was a turning point in his career.

> Being very systematic in sales and persistent is a key aspect in Europe. When you are a newcomer, every lead requires a lot of effort, and you really need great sales teams to make sure any hint that there could be an opportunity to close will be well looked after. What Vinod also mentioned during the interview was one of their European competitors offering very long delivery times, and how he was able to secure customers by proposing and delivering under very good delivery timelines. Sometimes, it just takes a small crack to get in, but the sales team needs to be on high alert and smart to move to leverage and convert.
>
> I also like the fact that being recognized as a leader in the industry has driven Phoenix and Vinod to make recommendations to UNICEF for technological advancements. Not only is it commendable, it also positions Phoenix as a respected and trusted business that can contribute to progress in the industry and also to the UNICEF programs.

Vigience successes: Markus's recipe for success in Europe

Markus's recipe for success is to detect one sponsor in a country, and then find the right go-to strategy with that partner, working on getting the price and other details right. It's about getting a soft referral from these sponsors when they detect Vigience can solve a problem for a specific company. They grew from there, one new customer at a time. This is the recipe that worked for Vigience.

He also mentioned that Denmark was a success for them. As it is a smaller market, they just needed a couple of customers to take on the product and then they could grow the market from there pretty fast.

Markus's recipe for success shows the power of a well-run channel partner/distribution program. In the same vein as the CleanSpace distribution channel recipe for success, this is about finding your sales champions within the channel partner or distributor, and working with them, training them and supporting them until the point that they start to refer you some business. And continuing to support them on their journey selling and recommending your product or solution. They need to be regularly updated, and you need to hear the types of objections they receive from their clients and help them get their first success. Once they start being success-ful and if you help them reach their sales quota with your product, they will keep referring your product or solution. And you need to be there for them in that learning curve.

The comment around the success in Denmark I quite like. I find it quite attractive when you can afford to pursue a core major market and you have a smaller, easier, faster market you set up in parallel. If you are able to do that, sometimes it means you can get a bit of revenue locked in while you work intensively in your core high-priority market. It's worth keeping this idea in mind, if a small market keeps surfacing in your industry.

Chapter 8

12 lessons learned

As I was reviewing all the challenges, successes and lessons learned from the CEOs and senior professionals interviewed for this book, I realized that these lessons were equally important. Lessons are best learnt when you need to listen to them and when they come at the right time for you.

If you are right at the start of your journey in Europe, there are certain lessons that are critical for you to know right now to minimize the risk of failure. If your business has been fairly active in Europe already, you may want to hear more 'advanced' lessons. So to make sure these lessons resonate with you and with the stage you are at in your business expansion in Europe, I have curated 12 lessons learnt and I have arranged them as follows:

- The two lessons that are important at the start.

- The lessons that make a difference between success and failure.

- The lessons that are good to know.

- If you've got cash to acquire your market position.

THE TWO LESSONS THAT ARE IMPORTANT AT THE START

When I reviewed the interviews, I realized that one of the important things is for a business to head in the right direction as they start their entry into the European market. Otherwise, they focus on the wrong market and spend money on activities that don't yield any revenue. Ultimately it results in years of investment for no return, or in a much longer start than initially planned. For businesses in the smaller end, it may have dramatic consequences.

Lesson #1: Go where your largest addressable market is and where there is a market appetite for your product

Joe L. triggered my attention on the first lesson I would like to share with you. When I asked him what he would do differently if he was to start again, he made two very interesting statements. First, he realized that looking at how many German customers the business now has, he should never have started in the UK. His conclusion is that they should have started where their largest total addressable market (TAM) was. It was Germany, and not the UK. TAM is the total market size if a company 'would aim for the moon'.[55]

Learning about your main target market as soon as possible and in as much depth as possible gets you faster and more significant results. Tom Mercer from Bean Ninjas on this topic even goes to the extent of saying: for the European market, besides UK, France and Germany, why bother? Those are his exact words.

---

55 This is a definition given in an article by EY Netherlands, published in 2018: 'Why top-down forecasting is a crucial exercise for startups.' www.ey.com/en_nl/ finance-navigator/why-top-down-forecasting-is-a-crucial-exercise-for-startups.

In absolute terms, Joe and Tom are right. However, in my experience, strategically for smaller businesses that need to quickly generate sales, sometimes having as a target a smaller, more accessible market may be useful to generate sales faster. It is often the case that the trio of large markets (UK, France and Germany) can take a bit of time to switch on. So I agree with focusing on the largest TAM, but an additional smaller market to work on in parallel can be an interesting option when you need fast sales.

As per Joe L.'s experience, companies from English-speaking countries tend to start with the UK 'naturally' as speaking the same language gives the illusion of proximity. There is an underlying expectation that it will be easier this way. This mistake is so common. Now that you have read about it, if you are from Australia, the US, Canada, South Africa or Singapore, please do not choose the UK as an export destination by default. It is a perilous exercise.

Proximity of languages creates an illusion that it will be easier; this is a lure. Markus experienced this. As a Swiss German, he thought: here we come Germany, my team and I speak German, I come from there. There was an expectation it would make it easier. This was not the case.

In my business, we use the TAM as a great indicator to determine the best potential countries for our customers. We usually like to select two top European countries. And to be sure that the focus is right and to make sure we can generate sales as fast as possible, we test 'the market appetite' in both top countries. This can only be determined by gathering feedback from key potential sales channels and prospective customers in the two countries. This is where we can quickly see which market will switch on first. We do that because we work with small and medium-sized companies that need a fast return on their investment in Europe. Even larger companies have an obligation to show results. Combining TAM and market appetite is a great combination to achieve sales faster.

Lesson #2: Sign your first deals and create your anchors in the European market

Initial successes and nice deals with the right target customers in the initial stages of market entry are vital to prove that there is a market for your product. It also gives confidence to investors that they can keep funding this venture. It gives product development teams confidence about the product. And most importantly it validates the market potential and helps project revenue. Therefore, these initial sales are critical to the future international success of businesses.

One of the most interesting learning experiences I heard during the interviews was the one of Markus with his business Vigience, when entering the DACH region.[56] His business has attempted twice to enter the European market and the second attempt was successful.

What Markus outlines in his interview is that they found it a lot harder than expected. They underestimated the effort it takes to break into the European market. Because they speak the language and Markus is a native of this region, they thought it would be much easier. The way the business sells and markets their product in Japan is quite different to Europe. What Markus and his team did in the first attempt is that he hired a marketing company to put together collateral and look after the web presence, as well as an online marketing campaign. And it didn't work that well.

Now what I find very interesting is how Markus changed the approach completely the second time around. He adopted a much leaner approach. He set the go to market strategy and took the business there. He wrote his website messaging, the collateral and the Power-Points. He realized he was the person who knew the product the best. In parallel he attended every sales call to learn from every customer, and to understand where the product did not fit into the European

---

56 DACH: acronym for D: Deutschland/Germany – A: Oesterreich/Austria –
    CH: Communaute Helvetique/Swizterland.

market needs. And gradually he adjusted their messaging and marketing to take into account this critical customer feedback.

When entering the European market, almost everything was new and different from their home market in Japan. They had different competitors, different expectations, different customers and different sales channels.

To achieve success, the main lessons that Markus shared with us are to be agile and be able to adjust messages and product features on the fly. It is not about heavy investment in marketing, or setting up local teams. It is about starting by listening to the customers' needs. Markus learnt in this exercise that you must adapt to the needs of your early adopters, because they are critical to your success in the European market.

Dr Alex Birrell of CleanSpace concurs with Markus's view on getting someone from the management team of the business involved in the sales calls. Here is what Alex says:

'It was a priority for the business to learn really quickly while entering the European market. A lot of the management team, in operations and also senior salespeople here in Australia, got involved. They were across the details and across the sales conversations, so that they could adjust on the fly. So often, the team was involved in the corporate customers' conversations and was there supporting technically, so that they could hear, learn and adjust.'

When asked about the early key reference sites won by CleanSpace, Alex Birrell underlines how much work goes into some of those. It's also not one person's job – it's a team effort so multiple people across different roles of the organization being completely aligned around getting this customer as a reference site across the line. This is according to Alex a real key to learning the business and the ability to be successful with large corporations in B2B.

Reflecting on these lessons learnt by both Markus and Alex, I really would like to underline the importance of being agile and persistent to win your first European customers, particularly as starting from scratch in a small business is very different to setting up a subsidiary overseas for a multinational. Funds are not unlimited. And there is no market awareness about the brand. This is also what Dr Tinazli mentioned, as he worked on the market entry of Fluxergy in Europe.

It also means you treat these 'anchor' customers like royalty. These customers are your advocates in your market, not because you are nice, but fundamentally because your product is solving a major problem for them. And no other product is doing that problem solving for them. That is why they are behind you and they will start to promote your product to their peers. Solid key opinion leaders that are ethical and professional won't put their reputation at risk if they don't believe in your product.

What's crucial when you start in Europe is to create loyalty. This is why these first customers deserve 'royalty' status and customer service – you need them to stay your customers. It took you a while as a newcomer to win them over, and you cannot afford to lose them!

THE LESSONS THAT MAKE A DIFFERENCE BETWEEN SUCCESS AND FAILURE

Lesson #3: A deep cultural understanding is what is going to bring you access to the information you need to make the right decisions to succeed

The cultural connection has been mentioned a couple of times by the interviewees. As a European, I take it as a given to take into consideration the cultural dimension while doing business. However, this is harder to apprehend as an outsider: 'you don't know what you don't know'. There are things I can see as a European that a non-Europeans cannot see.

Even in my own organization, I rely on insiders within each country to get the full picture and perspective on the business landscape.

Matt Harding says it very well as he traveled the world as a musician: many times he realized he made a fool of himself because of cultural faux-pas as an American. These lessons have helped him as a Chairman of Futramed for his dealings with the French market, one of which is worth sharing: **'To have respect for what you don't know about the culture that you're dealing with and you'll be interacting with.'** Matt Harding, having lived in Spain for many years and having the French market as target market, soon realized the role of social gatherings to get to know your French or Spanish counterparts. He took the time for it and realized it was worth it as a French doctor he was looking to create a strategic partnership with opened up to him to say that before he could do business with him, he first had to like him as a person. Talking about the private side of life is an important part of French culture as you build a partnership.

As strongly as Joe L. thinks that their technology speaks the international language of numbers and data does not lie, he also recognizes that 'people still buy from people, no matter how good your technology is'. He recognizes that only when they started to connect with local networks in their industry that things started to change for them.

At the practical level, CleanSpace's CEO mentioned the fact that they used a partner like Exportia to navigate languages and having access to the right information also helped to accelerate their success. She provides this advice about getting attuned to local markets:

'First of all, Europe is a great market – don't be put off by language. I think that's easily solved. Second, I find Europeans incredibly professional so there's actually a lot of service providers and partners that you can go with who have a lot more business affinity with an Australian way of doing business, so we found very sophisticated businesses.'

On this topic, Tom Mercer from Bean Ninjas also shared an interesting lesson that he learnt while interacting with the German market. As he was starting to make some headway with the German market, in a highly regulated industry such as accounting, he started to receive paper-based correspondence in registered letters from German authorities and he quickly realized even though he is a British citizen, based in the UK and in theory 'closer' to Germans than an American or an Australian business would be, that unless you are able to support a market in their own language, it's better not to venture in it.

Lesson #4: Hiring is strategic, risky and costly, so the decision to hire should be carefully considered

Now we know that hiring straight off the bat is not the way to go. We also learnt that it's better to understand in which European country you will have the most traction before you start hiring. This way you can make the right decision about the location to hire your first employee. I now would like to share the insight of Dr Alex Birrell about hiring in Europe; she clearly outlines how they started the hiring process and what milestones they achieved before they did. I think it's really interesting to see how having started to sell in a given European market puts you in a much better position when it's time to hire. You can use the network you have built while growing sales, and local industry candidates start coming to you.

Alex Birrell mentions that their very first recruitment was not right and they realized that they had the wrong strategy. So they rethought their strategy and partnered with a local specialist (Exportia). We used a local specialist to help us open up the markets. It gave us more focus and the languages that we needed. It gave us a lot more discipline around the preparation, investigation and research about how we went to market. The use of end-user reference sites, at the same time as setting up distribution, were key for us. It was a more methodical way of doing business.

I asked Alex when they had the confidence to hire. She said it was really when they had distribution that they relied on and they had key deployments into key reference sites. They actually had business happening there, and they had the confidence they had the model right and needed to do more of it. It became a lot easier to bring people to help them manage the market as opposed to setting the market up.

The other aspect about hiring that Alex highlights is: 'hiring small, not necessarily hiring large'. The more senior you hire, the more they think they are going to manage. And the difficulty when starting into a market is that you need to hire someone who will be the 'player coach'. It means someone who's going to do the customer selling and still work with distribution partners, and not just managing a team to do that on their behalf. They're doing management, making corporate decisions, but they're also building the business and doing the sales as well. It's key to have that role.

On the topic of hiring, I found also quite interesting the experience of Tom Mercer from Bean Ninjas. As a service business, it's a completely different ballgame.

According to Tom, the main lesson was to hire in advance, particularly for them as a service business. If they do not have the people they cannot generate sales. It takes him about three months to get to the point where he can leave the service delivery with them. So he learnt to plan ahead. In a start-up position, it's hard to balance cash flow. You don't want to hire too early, but it is so much worse if you hire late, because you get caught. And for him that would mean being caught doing the day to day rather than focusing on developing the business and having more of a strategic focus.

In most European countries, a dismissal is quite costly in terms of indemnity (I have seen up to €250,000 indemnity for a senior manager). But more importantly, making the wrong recruitment can at best slow your growth or in the worst case can sink your boat.

I also think that hiring a junior to start in a market has a lot of value. It's less risky. If you are a dynamic business, you may have more to offer than a traditional, well-established business. Younger people may be attracted to more innovative businesses, whereas more senior sales-people will find it harder to switch for some unknown.

Lesson #5: The channels are equally as important as the product

One of the things that came up as a critical success factor in Europe was the sales channels and how they were used to drive sales. Markus of Vigience's statement is very striking:

'The go to market channel and who you market with (your partner) is equally as important as the product.'

On the topic of sales channels, it was also interesting to hear the learning of Joe L. He thought that when they started, if they had sold through channel partners first instead of hiring, they would have grown faster and would have had more customers and more revenue by now.

It highlights the importance of sales channels as a key strategy to succeed in Europe.

Markus said that he realized he could leverage the power and presence of the CRM software vendors that his product was connect-ing to, namely Salesforce and Microsoft. When he made his second attempt at entering the European market, he decided to go with just one partner (Salesforce). That enabled him with a very lean team to really commit to this partner and to focus all his attention on one partner and on getting their sales team understanding their offer really well.

Joe L. says that if a business thinks about the amount of investment they are willing to make and it's relatively small, and there's just not enough money, then you need to find a way to be bigger. In the case of his business, finding consulting partners or technology partners that are big and being part of that, and spending time and effort there, is the way to be bigger.

The dimension that Joe is highlighting here is interesting, not only from the investment side, but also from a credibility standpoint. If the business is relatively small and you are targeting €2 billion companies, it's not ideal to go alone and it will take much longer to be successful.

Joe L. said: 'If I was the CEO now of a company similar to my company as it was 20 years ago, I definitely would try to sell through partners.'

To be fair he recognizes that at the time their offer was not truly software; there was code, but at the time it would have been complex for a partner to sell and implement. However, Joe still thinks that at the time having established some referral partners paid on a commission, he would have done well. He thinks that he would have had more customers, he thinks that instead of growing 40% a year they would probably have grown 80% a year. Business would have grown earlier, more and faster. It was not his decision at the time not to implement partners.

Distribution is a partnership: distributors have their own business priorities so you must be ready to be agile

Now let's take a manufacturer's angle on distribution with the Clean-Space experience.

I asked Alex why some distributors in some regions were successful and in other regions distributors were not that successful. Alex puts it down to the actual company personality. It may be their pace. Sometimes when they pick a distributor, maybe their customer base isn't the right one for the business, but you don't always know that until you start working with them.

A distributor is just like any other business. They go through growth phases, they have changing management. They are changing strategy, they might be doing other things, like a merger and acquisition, and so they might be a bit distracted. Sometimes they are not successful initially and become successful, or they start by being successful in the first years and then something happens, like a restructure, and they take their eyes off the ball. **With distribution, it's never set and forget.**

With your distribution channel, you need to be looking out for the right partner. What's motivating them? What's distracting them? What changes are coming up in their business that may impact your business as well? When you pick up a distributor or you're mapping a market for distribution channels, you need to work out what's best for your business, and what's best for the business may change over time as well. These channels may change, so you always have to be agile.

Alex mentions what CleanSpace did wrong at the start. They were not actively investigating the distribution channels; they should have researched them more. That means as well that they were initially unable to drive the partnership. That was understandable as they were new to the market and they did not know what they did not know.

Going forward, they do a lot more research about distributors. They are a lot more active in how they prepare, and how they investigate them. They are also more proactive in the way they set them up, and how they manage them on an ongoing basis. Alex's lesson is that any company doing that for the first time has to be prepared to fail and learn from it very fast, and adjust.

Setting up distributors is a key strategy to succeed in the European market. It offers a faster footprint as non-European entrants can directly integrate a local ecosystem – the one of their partner. It gives them readily available access to their ideal customer base. As a new entrant into Europe, and particularly targeting large corporates, partnering with a large distributor or a partner offers much better access to key accounts. It accelerates sales and negates the immediate need to hire a large local team.

Identifying the right partners takes a thoughtful mapping of partners for each market. Then a selection process, and then the work is just starting! It is now time, as Alex said, to make sure that your distribution partner does not take their eyes off the ball.

Lesson #6: Making the most of a post-pandemic environment

In my interviews, I asked how each business had been impacted by the pandemic and how it changed their business.

For the healthcare businesses that were interviewed it either really accelerated their growth (for CleansSpace) or it put on hold some of their progress. For example, Futramed trials were put on hold for a while. Phoenix was impacted by a reduced amount of government and international institution funding, as all fundings were oriented towards combatting the pandemic. In healthcare, it also created confusion in the market. So many new players entered this market, knowing very little about the complexities.

It was interesting to hear from Dr Tinazli that he really had to put new potential distributors on the grill to understand if they really knew anything about healthcare. A lot of European distributors have sold consumables to hospitals during the pandemic, but did it make them understand how it actually is to sell to a clinical team? I can share as per my own experience with our customers, that as a fact, they don't have a clue. So there is a little bit of special care to put into selecting potential partners in European markets if you are in healthcare, a bit more than usual. In other words, **one of the short-term pandemic lessons is: if you are in healthcare and are looking for European distributors, don't just sign up the first distributors that pretend they sell to hospitals. You will really have to check this.**

The software and professional services businesses did not feel as much of an impact. Markus of Vigience took advantage of suddenly gaining the ability to interact with European customers in very productive online meetings from Tokyo. And CleanSpace noticed the same, with their sales teams delivering online demos and embracing a fully online sales process during the pandemic. Others had to put on hold some of their business development activities because of the lack of events and face-to-face interactions.

Whether it had a positive or a negative impact on the business, whether the pandemic has been an accelerator or an impediment, it has forced several transformational changes I believe businesses need to make to continue to grow and futureproof in Europe.

One aspect is to continue digitization. The adjustment of your sales process to an online sales process is critical. There is a general acceptance now that 100% face-to-face meetings are not always needed. European multinationals have adopted this practice and now tend to favor it. For health and safety precautions, some of them have even minimized numbers of visits from external companies. We know that a lot of products can be demonstrated online. Many sales meetings can be held online. You can deal with many different European countries in one single day online.

So I think it's important to look at every stage in your sales process and check what can be done remotely. If you think about your own sales process, in the presales phase, what can be done online, remotely, and the same applies during the conversion from a lead to a sale. Then in the aftersales, for the implementation of the product. In B2B it may require an installation and a deployment. At every step of the sales process, you need to ask yourself what can or should be done remotely.

Here is one of the templates we use in my business to describe a B2B sales process.

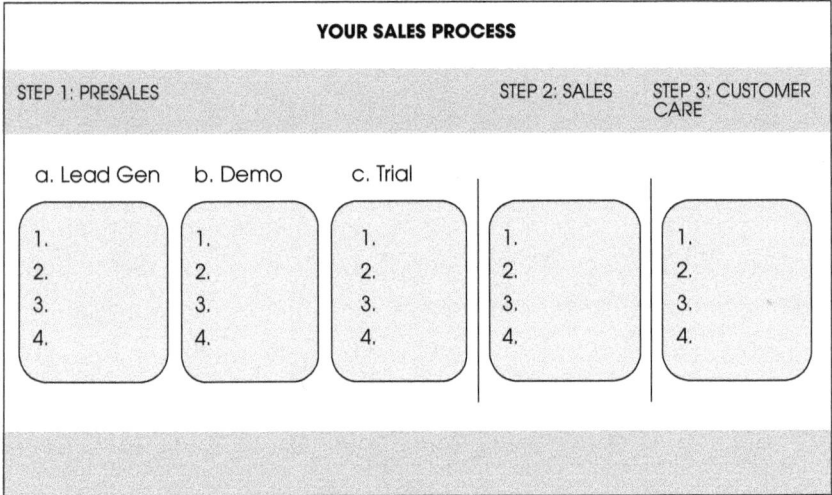

YOUR SALES PROCESS				
STEP 1: PRESALES			STEP 2: SALES	STEP 3: CUSTOMER CARE
a. Lead Gen	b. Demo	c. Trial		
1. 2. 3. 4.	1. 2. 3. 4.	1. 2. 3. 4.	1. 2. 3. 4.	1. 2. 3. 4.

In presales, a lot of the lead-generation phase can be done through online campaigns, on social media. We conduct a lot of our lead-generation campaigns over the phone only. In a market entry stage in a new country, trade shows are not the only way to go. Lead-generation campaigns are great and can be done remotely and in a cost-effective way.

The product demonstrations can be done via videos that you can record and share; they can also be done in a video call.

When it comes to a trial, it is critical for the potential customer to be trained on the product remotely, and not to always have a technician come on site.

Lesson #7: European trade shows

What I have seen repeatedly and what the companies I interviewed for this book also mentioned were major European trade shows. Businesses entering the European market repeatedly mention that a major

European show they would go to every year or two would be where they would make the most important European connections.

Phoenix and Fluxergy, as medical device companies, mentioned Medica as their flagship show, where significant contacts were made. Vinod of Phoenix mentioned that this show was the foundation to major and long-term business connections. Dr Tinazli mentioned that Medica for him, as a new business starting in the European market, gave him a good impression of what the market wants and needs. With the 40 initial meetings he organized at Medica he could really get a good feel for it. Dr Alex Birrell, of CleanSpace, mentioned A+A for the safety industry as being the place where a lot of strategic relationships were formed.

In my business, we place a lot of emphasis on shows as companies enter the European market and we need to rapidly build a pipeline. One of the fastest ways to build exposure and a solid pipeline of opportunities is exhibiting at trade shows. If you select the majors in your industry and you prepare your presence really well, it will accelerate your success. And being a consistent exhibitor helps you build your credibility over time. The most important part is to conduct a lead-generation campaign three to six months ahead of the show. This way, you can channel all the interested parties to a meeting at the show. And the contacts that have been really hard to reach, you can increase your success rate by inviting them to come along.

Reflecting on Phoenix's presence at trade shows, Vinod made an interesting comment. While they are successfully exhibiting at Medica, and will continue to do so, he thinks that investing in a presence at a smaller, more specialized conference where his potential end-users go may be a very smart investment. He would do that in a selected country he would like to focus on and grow. He thinks that by triggering the interest of doctors directly in these specialized conferences and asking them where they buy from will allow him to select better distributors. It will allow him to also incentivize distributors to start distributing his product.

When a doctor shows interest, they can call in the local distributor to ask for a demonstration. When a doctor with a high profile, like a key opinion leader, can call their distributor and ask for a Phoenix CPAP instead of what they have been traditionally selling, it creates market traction. And it is then easier to push Phoenix specifications to the Ministry of Health in that country.

Indeed, very large trade shows like Medica and A+A are mostly visited by European distributors looking for new products. And they have a lot of value for this reason.

However, exhibiting at a national, more specialized 'end-user focused' conference, you can ensure that the distributors present will be targeting the right market. It will save you a lot of time. In addition, it will trigger their interest to work with you, as you are talking to their customers. It changes the entire dynamic.

In the last five years, we have experimented with digital congresses, and we have never achieved the same level of engagement or connections that a face-to-face show has brought. Choosing a show carefully is the underlying condition to success. And the best way to do so is to detect where your customers go. If you just focus on the congress or the trade show where your target goes year after year, you just keep exhibiting at this show and keep improving your presence.

One of the lessons I have personally learnt is to plan well around compliance with General Data Protection Regulation (GDPR) laws. It is really important to check with the show organizers what data they are collecting at registration and what that means to you. Prior to GDPR, you could take someone's business card or scan their badge and just load them into your CRM and subscribe them to your email list. That is not the case anymore.

European customers are very familiar with their right to keep their data private. Spamming via email and phone calls has increased exponentially, so it's really important to check with the organizers what protocol is in place with GDPR, and also to take into account your visitors' choices and to ask them for consent to collect their data.

Lesson #8: Sales agents

Tom Arbanas of Du-Co shared an interesting lesson with us about sales agents. When they acquired a competitor, they inherited sales agency contracts in Europe. They knew what the sales agents were paid in the US (called manufacturers' reps) and they were familiar with the usual business model of sales agents and their contractual arrangements. When they acquired their competitor they found out that the sales agents' contracts included unusual costs such as office and travel expenses on top of the commission. Therefore Du-Co had to renegotiate these agreements with the European sales agent in question.

European sales agents are a great way to expand your regional presence in each European country. They are usually paid on a commission-only basis. They are not easy to find and they are mostly one-person businesses. But there are also larger agencies with several reps. They are more common in certain industries in comparison to others.

There is a lot of value in setting sales agents up. They already have daily contact with your regional dealers or distributors, and they know and visit local customers or end-users on a regular basis. It is a great way to deepen your regional presence. It gives a business the ability to have their product or solution presented and introduced every single week to potential customers. Non-European businesses need not worry about having a local subsidiary or local employment laws. Having a European sales agent network is a powerful way to accelerate sales.

Lesson #9: Packaging

Two manufacturers, Fluxergy and Phoenix, mentioned the importance of packaging their products well when shipping to European markets. It happened to both companies that products were damaged as they landed in Europe. Making sure that the product arrives intact and without damage is the minimum you would expect. And so these companies had to rethink their packaging to protect their products during transport. Phoenix even used the services of a packaging specialist. They even went to the extent of reducing the size of the user manuals that go with the products – they focused on more pictures and less text.

Packaging is a critical part of exporting at the moment, for several reasons. First, the cost of freight has increased dramatically, and avoiding damage during transport is critical so you don't have to pay the cost of shipping a replacement product. In addition, it is worth thinking about packaging from a weight perspective as well to enable optimum transport costs.

The other dimension is to adopt sustainable packaging. In recent years, European distributors have asked their suppliers to demonstrate how they are minimizing their impact on the environment. Packaging needs to minimize the use of plastic and be made of sustainable material. By 2030, the European Union wants all packaging available in its market to be recyclable.[57] The sustainability dimension is now critical in the European Union, and exporters to Europe must take into account three priorities:

- reduce packaging and packaging waste

---

57 'Communication From The Commission To The European Parliament, The Council, The European Economic And Social Committee And The Committee Of The Regions. A new Circular Economy Action Plan For a Cleaner and More Competitive Europe,' March 11, 2020. Paragraph 3.3. eur-lex.europa.eu/legal-content/EN/TXT/?qid=1583933814386&url=COM:2020:98:FIN.

- drive design for reuse and recyclability of packaging

- reduce the complexity of packaging materials, including the number of materials and polymers used.

Lesson #10: Don't small businesses use dashboards?

As part of this interviewing exercise, and as a part of my experience with Exportia, I realized that businesses keep very little track of how they perform and their progress into the European market. Defining a sales target when you first enter a market does not really make sense as you find your feet; it can be very dissuasive for a sales team to start to pressure them with a target when they are just trying to understand the market, the local customer, and as they are finding out the key players and distributors in the market. However, it's always good to keep some achievable objectives in mind. These achievable goals can be articulated around activity and milestones, and implementing these milestones is what will generate sales at the end of the day. Let me give you an example: talking to 20 qualified customers in the next six months and to five major potential distributors should give you great feedback and give you a preliminary idea on what it will take you to build a solid pipeline of leads to then generate sales. These are simple goals.

On the other hand, it's good for teams to be systematic in their recording of their progress against these goals. Having a central repository of this information in a CRM, in a monthly sales report or in a project management system is often overlooked. What I have found is that in the domestic market this is often comprehensively captured, but for overseas customers it's a bit looser. It's important to have tight reporting and accurately capture the activity and progress against these simple goals.

Lesson #11: The importance of writing processes to scale

The last good to know lesson comes unsurprisingly from a service business perspective. None of the interviewees talked about the importance of writing systems and processes to be able to scale a business internationally, except Tom Mercer of Bean Ninjas. I think it is a good lesson to share equally with service businesses, software companies and manufacturers. When you scale internationally, you need to make sure there is consistency in the way your product is delivered, in the way your customers are trained, and in the way your sales process is delivered by your sales team worldwide.

Tom Mercer mentioned that they did pause their marketing activities for a while, and they used that pause to write every single process that was needed to enable them to scale internationally. He mentioned that when you start, you realize how many more processes are needed! He even had to articulate in a visual chart the different processes of the business. And in his experience, this was the turning point in what enabled them to scale. Instead of him spending hours and hours with a new team member training them and going through everything and even having to micromanage them, he now provides field training on all these different processes. And now a new team member can hit the ground running in a much shorter timeframe. They even rewrote the processes about a year after, to enable local managers to train their own team using the same system.

I think this is such a great thing to do when expanding into the European market. At Exportia, when we start working for a new customer as an outsourced sales team based in Europe, and our customer's HQ is based in Australia, in the US or in Asia, we usually spend a lot of time creating these processes with our customers, to make sure the sales process we follow is right and the customer we target has the right profile. We also want to know what information can be shared and cannot be shared, and how. The better these processes are outlined, the better we can perform as a sales team. Micromanagement is counterproductive, in that it discourages initiative and learning of the local market.

Over the years, we have also seen a disconnect between the European team and the headquarters. It was often because the European team felt isolated, they did not know where to get answers for their customers or whom to ask; it often resulted in frustration.

Good and simple processes enable your European team to have enough autonomy, while being aligned with the rest of the business. It makes your overseas organization more efficient as well.

Lesson #12: Lessons learnt when acquiring a European business

The experience of the US company Du-Co is fascinating. As outlined earlier in the book, Du-Co had a very peculiar entry into the European market. They acquired their main competitor and it instantly gave them an increased footprint in the European market. They instantly acquired new customers in Europe and added turnover.

However, as they started to dig further into the deals that were signed with European customers by the previous owners, they realized that the pricing in Europe was not great for business. And in the end, they had to implement a massive price increase to restore profitability. So, they lost a few customers, and it was not as good an additional European footprint as they initially thought. On top of that, and as mentioned in the lesson learned around sales agents, they had to terminate the sales agencies' contracts as they were too expensive for the turnover generated. Du-Co had to pay travel and office expenses, when it is normal practice to pay European sales agents on a commission on sales only model.

If you are contemplating acquiring a European business or a business that has quite a good footprint in Europe, it is important to know precisely what these European customers are worth, and to assess if they are going to stay when you acquire them. A real insight into these customers pre-acquisition is important. Most merger and acquisition projects are run by the big four, by lawyers and accountants, which is a good and a bad thing. As business owners of small and medium-sized companies, you have a good understanding of your market. The seller may not disclose a lot of information about its customers and its market to every company that is showing interest in buying. In addition, you may have limited time during the due diligence process. So it's important to ask the right questions.

If I was to assess a business for acquisition, I would use my 7 Pillar frame-work. We use this framework in everything we do. Particularly when we assess a business's capability to export to Europe, but also when we get trained about their sales strategy. We also use these 7 Pillars when defining a strategy. Very naturally these pillars fit very well in the case of providing a framework to ask questions in the context of a potential acquisition.

Exportia 7 Pillars	Possible questions	What you are trying to find out
Product	Is their product compliant in the European market?	Are they just a me-too product?
	How is their price compared to European competitors?	How easy or hard will it be to grow?
	Do they know their European competitors?	
	What is their unique positioning?	

Exportia 7 Pillars	Possible questions	What you are trying to find out
Customers	What is the ideal customer profile of this business? What is their typical problem and how does the company's product solve this problem? How many of these ideal customers do they have in Europe? How long is the customer retention? Have they had new customers lately? What's their profile? Which customers are the most profitable? Are they selling to any large European multinational? Which ones? Are they selling to any governments in Europe? Which ones?	How valuable is their customer base? How sticky are their customers? Are they selling to their target?
Country	In which European country do they have the most success and why? How is the turnover split per country?	Is there any significant success in any European country that could be leveraged in other countries?
Channels	Do they use distribution channels? Solely, or do they also sell direct? How many distributors do they have per country? In how many European countries do they have distribution partners? Do they have exclusive agreements? Any KPIs to retain exclusivity? When did they last train a European distributor? What type of reporting do they provide to distributors?	Are their distribution channels working for them? Any potential for improvements? Are they stuck with distribution contracts, where the distributors are not performing?
Marketing	How do you think their brand is known in Europe? How do they measure it? What works well for them in terms of marketing in Europe?	Any improvements to be made in their marketing? What to stop and reconsider?

Exportia 7 Pillars	Possible questions	What you are trying to find out
Team	What is the profile of their sales team? In which European country are they based? How is their team spread in Europe? How many languages are spoken by their European team? What technical, management, sales backgrounds do they have? How are they paid?	What is the dynamic in the team culturally and from the geographical point of view? What is the real ability of the team to sell to major markets? Are they pretending to sell successfully to a country when they are not? The bonus system is a good way to measure how the team is managed and performance measured. How well has this team done?
Dashboards	Which CRM system do they use? Since when? How many contacts are there in this database? What percentage of the sales team is using it daily? How do you comply with GDPR?	Will their systems accurately provide you with access to customers?

In addition, there are very good survey companies that can provide qualitative information. They can be very effective in gathering qualitative data about customers and customer experiences.

Let's wrap it up

I have given you plenty of reasons to choose Europe now and to persist in Europe as a high-tech business. I have shared how there are right now opportunities in the European market for businesses in robotics, AI and 5G to **support European companies in their digital transformation**. The fight against climate change is now accelerating, allowing plenty of **green technology companies** in that space to help businesses reduce their carbon footprint. There are initiatives to **modernize European healthcare** systems and secure the supply of medical devices.

We have seen that we live in an ever-changing environment, and that we have to be agile, shift and change to adapt constantly to new dynamics. My own take away from this book is that non-European businesses entering or active in Europe need to keep it real. In an ever-changing environment, good old basics work wonders: for example, listen to European customers and understand their needs before you try to sell to them.

The essence of these stories is that all the participants that succeeded have listened to European customers and worked hand in hand with them to understand their needs and issues and to see how their solution could solve them. We saw this when Markus mentioned that he was on every call, when Vinod invited a Swiss expert to come in to their factory and asked for honest feedback, when Alex said the management team was on deck and actively listening. They have all admitted mistakes, so you have to accept that from the get-go. They have all transformed from these learnings and have adapted to customer feedback to fit the market needs.

They have understood that English could only take them so far, and they saw the shift as soon as they were able to have European support. We saw this when Alex started to work with us at Exportia, when Joe recruited in France to support his European effort. We also saw that when Markus, as a Swiss German, was really well equipped to enter the DACH as a native speaking the language, he had this asset in place that not many non-European businesses have when they start. But what he realized in his second attempt was that hiring straight away was probably not the best way, and that is what Alex mentioned as well. She realized that they first had to know where the market traction was, get a few deals under their belt and understand the market before it was time to hire to support further expansion.

In my business, we are very used to setting up distribution networks Europe-wide and we observe every day the acceleration effect it has on sales as it gives access to key customers for our clients. I was pleased to hear Markus, Joe and Alex found it to be strategic for their success in Europe. It enabled them to access bigger ecosystems than if they were going alone. And let's keep in mind, distribution and channel partners are not set and forget, as Alex said. It requires constant management and drive from you.

Have an open mind, and immerse yourself in this European world of opportunities. You now have plenty of information in your hands. Peers have generously shared their lessons and shown you the pathway to European success. I was honored to be your guide on your reading journey in the European landscape and to add my 20 years' experience to it.

Now succeed!

What's next in your European journey?

Now I am curious, where are you at in your journey in the European market? Are you just at the start? Or quite advanced? Maybe you and your team just had an attempt, and you are not quite happy about the outcome yet?

Whatever stage you are in, remember it's okay to make mistakes as long as you transform them into learnings. The goal of this book was really to demonstrate that others have done it before you. It was also important to showcase that the European opportunity is big right now for businesses like yours in advanced manufacturing, machinery, automation, in green technology and energy, in cloud computing, software for any industry vertical, and in agricultural technology, biotechnology, lab and medical devices.

Our pan-European team at Exportia takes pride in bringing success to non-European businesses like yours from Australia, New Zealand, the US, Canada, and the entire APAC region. We love to work with businesses that want to scale in Europe, come with an open mind and want acceleration. They know that there is only so much they can do without local support.

We would love you to join the cohort of businesses in high-tech sectors for which Exportia has accelerated sales in Europe. Contact us today to see how we can help you grow sales in Europe.

www.exportia.global

Thank yous

I would like to first and foremost thank my mentor Andrew Griffiths. When I was dreaming out loud with Andrew about the third book that I really would like to write, I told him what would be amazing would be to interview companies in tech sectors from all around the world. Their journeys would be so interesting. As I put this wish out there, Andrew's enthusiasm and drive was instrumental in giving me the confidence that it was actually possible! Had he not given me that positive signal, I would probably not have gathered all my courage for this international scouting exercise.

I am so thankful for the interviewees' time and honesty. I have thoroughly enjoyed the interviews and hearing their stories. It was so interesting and exciting to hear them tell their stories that I had to remind myself to keep my mouth shut and not interject. I cannot tell you how much I enjoyed conducting these interviews. I would like to warmly thank the interviewees: Dr Alex Birrell, Markus Stierli, Joe L, Vinod Narayanan, Matt Harding, Tom Arbanas, Tom Mercer and Dr Ali Tinazli for their time and for sharing their valuable experiences. Sharing your experiences will inspire, reassure, trigger and spark a light for exporters into the European market from around the world. I am forever grateful for your generosity.

Special thanks to Ralf Meyer, a long-term and esteemed business connection who kindly introduced me to Joe and Markus. Thanks to Jim Blair for his introduction to Tom as well.

Scott, thank you for letting me stay by the riverside to complete a big part of this book.

Thanks to Gilbert Casamajou for the wonderful illustrations.

Thank you to my excellent team at Exportia, whose support while I am in writing mode guarantees the top-notch service our clients deserve.

I thank my favorite people for their support, because for the third time, the book writing process means I have less time for them. Maya, mon cœur, merci de ton soutien inconditionnel du haut de tes bientôt 16 ans. Nik, my love, thank you for your unconditional love and support – they are priceless.

Would you like to share your European export story?

Maybe some of these stories resonated with you and your journey in Europe? If you liked what you read and would like to share your export stories in the European market, I would love to hear from you as I would like to continuously collect and showcase export stories:

community@exportia.global

About the author

Ever since she can remember, Christelle has been immersed in multiple European cultures through her family environment, where several languages were spoken, shaping her multicultural business mind. From there, she developed a deep love for pan-European business, leading her to found Exportia in 2006 as she migrated from France to Australia. This marks her third book. Her second book, *The 4 Steps to Generate Your First Million Euros in Sales*, a proven methodology to scale businesses in Europe, won the Best Australian Business Book Award in the Sales & Communication category in 2020.

Christelle serves as the Managing Director of Exportia, which provides European business development services to non-European B2B manufacturing and technology companies. Her business operates across Europe and maintains offices in Paris and Sydney, working with businesses globally, including Australia, New Zealand, the Asia-Pacific, the US, and Canada. Together with her team, they have guided over one hundred businesses to the European market, developing a 4-Step Framework and tailored tools for technology companies across various industry sectors to successfully scale in Europe. Exportia has a proven track record in scaling non-European businesses to their first million Euros and beyond.

Her career began at IBM Paris, where she looked after large corporate customers. However, she decided to pursue her passion for international business and focus on small businesses.

Christelle is also an international speaker, delivering workshops, keynotes, and masterclasses worldwide, both in person and online. Drawing from her experience and hard work in export journeys, she speaks on various topics including navigating the European market, high-performing European distribution networks, hiring in Europe, reaching scale Europe-wide, and breaking down barriers to growth. She is particularly passionate about helping technology companies build their capability to export to Europe for long-term success, having delivered workshops, masterclasses, and keynotes to over 200 non-European small and medium-sized businesses, predominantly in the technology sector, in recent years.

If you enjoyed reading this book and want to know more about Christelle's work and her business, **Exportia**, here are a few pages to explore, stay in touch and reach out.

Exp𝗈rtia®

We want to help *YOUR* company expand in Europe

At Exportia, we are a passionate team of European Sales Managers, Multilingual Lead Generators and Project Managers who have a track record in taking non-European small and medium-sized businesses to their first million euros in sales ... and far beyond.

We are ready to work with your team, whether you are at the start of your European journey or already well established.

To contact Christelle and her team today, email christelle.damiens@exportia.com.au

www.exportia.global

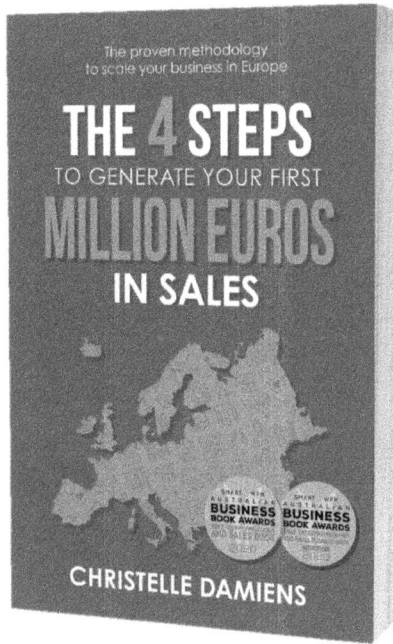

The proven methodology
to scale your business in Europe

THE 4 STEPS
TO GENERATE YOUR FIRST
MILLION EUROS
IN SALES

BUSINESS BUSINESS
BOOK AWARDS BOOK AWARDS

CHRISTELLE DAMIENS

If you liked this book, here is another of Christelle Damiens' books

The 4 Steps to Generate Your First Million Euros in Sales lays out the methodology that has been developed by Christelle following her twenty years of corporate sales experience and work with European distributors. This powerful framework has been proven with over hundred non-European businesses entering or further expanding into Europe.

Christelle's second book *The 4 Steps to Generate Your First Million Euros in Sales* won the **2020 Australian Business Book Award** in Communications, and is an **Amazon Best Seller**.

The 4 Steps to Generate Your First Million Euros in Sales is available for sale on Amazon and shop at:
www.exportia.global

Engage Christelle as a Speaker for your next event

Christelle is an international business speaker. She has delivered presentations to more than 250 small and medium-sized businesses internationally.

She delivers keynotes, workshops, webinars, and masterclasses. She can deliver talks in English, French and German.

Christelle talks about the following topics:
- Export and international expansion
- International expansion in the European market
- B2B international sales
- Global growth for start-ups
- European sales for technology-based products
- Software & services
- Distribution & channel partners networks

For more information about engaging Christelle to present at your next in-person or virtual event, email:
info@christelledamiens.com

www.christelledamiens.com

For media interviews with Christelle

**Christelle is regularly featured by the media internationally.
She can talk with authority on the following topics:**

- Opportunities in the European market
- Why Small Businesses from non-EU countries should consider Europe
- Current European market conditions
- Doing business in the multilingual multicultural Europe
- Start-ups going global
- Women in international business
- Benefits of exporting for small business
- Tech exports, advanced manufacturing exports
- Medical devices exports

If you'd like to interview Christelle about any of the above, or
her latest book, please email: **info@christelledamiens.com**

www.christelledamiens.com

sky NEWS BUSINESS   DYNAMIC | BUSINESS   AMT AUSTRALIAN MANUFACTURING TECHNOLOGY MAGAZINE

Le nouvel Economiste   france info   DYNAMIC EXPORT a smarter way to trade

Exportia services to government departments from around the world

Christelle and her team work with various government departments from around the world. They collaborate with organisations that are supporting start-ups, small and medium enterprises in their international growth, particularly in Europe.

Exportia provides the following services to government departments:

- Export trainings for small businesses
- Online events
- Trade events
- Coaching
- Trade delegation and trade show programs
- B2B Business matching

Contact Christelle and her team today to discuss these services, email: **christelle.damiens@exportia.com.au**

www.exportia.global

FREE access to more resources and content about European market

To access FREE resources about the European market, or get support, you can:

Download sales tools

Register for free tutorials

Watch videos

Watch webinar recordings

Register for the next Exportia event

Visit the **Resources** section of the Exportia website:
www.exportia.global

www.ingramcontent.com/pod-product-compliance
Lightning Source LLC
Chambersburg PA
CBHW040915210326
41597CB00030B/5089